S0-ARW-693

WORKBOOK

Focus on Grammar

A **BASIC** Course for Reference and Practice

SECOND EDITION

Samuela Eckstut

Longman

FOCUS ON GRAMMAR WORKBOOK: A BASIC COURSE FOR REFERENCE AND PRACTICE

Copyright © 2000, 1994 by Addison Wesley Longman, Inc.
A Pearson Education Company.
All rights reserved.
No part of this publication may be reproduced,
stored in a retrieval system, or transmitted
in any form or by any means, electronic, mechanical,
photocopying, recording, or otherwise,
without the prior permission of the publisher.

Pearson Education, 10 Bank Street, White Plains, NY 10606

Editorial director: Allen Ascher
Executive editor: Louisa Hellegers
Director of design and production: Rhea Banker
Development editor: Lise Minovitz
Production manager: Alana Zdinak
Managing editor: Linda Moser
Senior production editor: Virginia Bernard
Production editor: Christine Lauricella
Senior manufacturing manager: Patrice Fraccio
Manufacturing supervisor: David Dickey
Cover design: Rhea Banker
Text design adaptation: Rainbow Graphics
Text composition: Rainbow Graphics
Illustrator: Dave Sullivan

ISBN: 0–201–34687–7

2 3 4 5 6 7 8 9 10—BAH—05 04 03 02 01 00

CONTENTS

ABOUT THE AUTHOR

Samuela Eckstut has taught ESL and EFL for twenty years, in the United States, Greece, Italy, and England. Currently she is teaching at Boston University, Center for English Language and Orientation Programs (CELOP). She has authored or co-authored numerous texts for the teaching of English, notably *What's in a Word? Reading and Vocabulary Building*; *In the Real World*; *First Impressions*; *Beneath the Surface*; *Widely Read*; and *Finishing Touches*.

THE PRESENT AFFIRMATIVE OF *BE*

1 AFFIRMATIVE OF *BE*

Complete the conversations. Use **I am, you are, he is, she is, it is, we are,** *or* **they are.**

1. **A:** How are you?

   B: _____ I am _____ fine.

2. **A:** How are you and your wife?

   B: _____ fine.

3. **A:** How is your daughter?

   B: _____ fine.

4. **A:** How is your son?

   B: _____ fine.

5. **A:** How are your mother and father?

   B: _____ fine.

6. **A:** Where are you?

   B: _____ in the garden.

7. **A:** Where is the sandwich?

   B: _____ on the table.

8. **A:** Where are the keys?

   B: _____ in the car.

9. **A:** Where is Mrs. Robinson?

   B: _____ in the office.

10. **A:** Where am I?

    B: _____ at school.

2 SUBJECT PRONOUNS

Change the underlined words. Use **he**, **she**, **it**, **we**, *or* **they**.

Hello. I am Rocco. My last name is Marciano. ~~My last name~~ is an Italian name. My family
^{It} over strike — **It** above "My last name", **1.**

and I are from Italy. Now <u>my family and I</u> live here. Anna is my mother. <u>My mother</u> is
2. ... **3.**

from a village in Abruzzi. <u>The village</u> is very small. Silvano is my father. <u>My father</u> is from
4. ... **5.**

Naples. <u>Naples</u> is a big city in the south of Italy. I am from Naples, too.
6.

My parents are in Italy now. <u>My parents</u> are on vacation. I am at home with my sisters.
7.

<u>My sisters and I</u> are not happy alone. <u>My sisters</u> are always angry with me. My brother
8. ... **9.**

is lucky. <u>My brother</u> is not at home. <u>My brother</u> is at college. <u>The college</u> is far away.
10. ... **11.** ... **12.**

3 AFFIRMATIVE OF *BE*

Write true statements. Use words from columns **A**, **B**, *and* **C** *in each sentence.*

A	B	C
I		at home
My best friend		at work
My mother	am	cold
My father	is	friendly
My teacher	are	happy
My parents		heavy
My classmates		hot
		in love
		late
		short
		tall
		thin
		worried
		a student
		a nice person
		nice people

1.   I am a student.

2. _____

3. _____

4. _____

5. _____

6. _____

7. _____

8. _____

9. _____

10. _____

4 CONTRACTIONS OF AFFIRMATIVE STATEMENTS WITH *BE*

Write the conversations in full form.

1. **A:** It's eight o'clock. It is eight o'clock.

   B: Oh, no! We're late. Oh, no! We are late.

2. **A:** We're here.

   B: That's wonderful.

3. **A:** Your food's on the table.

   B: Good! I'm hungry.

4. **A:** Charlie's in love with Linda.

   B: But she's engaged!

5. **A:** I'm sorry about the window.

   B: That's okay.

6. **A:** I think the picture's beautiful.

   B: You're kidding! It's terrible.

7. **A:** I'm so glad to be here.

   B: We're glad, too.

5 CONTRACTIONS OF AFFIRMATIVE STATEMENTS WITH *BE*

Write the conversations with contractions.

1. **A:** It is eight o'clock. It's eight o'clock.

   B: Oh, no! We are late. Oh, no! We're late.

2. **A:** That woman is beautiful.

   B: She is my wife.

3. **A:** Hello. I am Nancy Marks.

   B: Hi. My name is Hank Stewart.

4. **A:** They are nice people.

   B: But they are so boring.

(continued on next page)

5. A: My daughter is in the hospital. _____

    B: We are sorry to hear that. _____

6. A: We are glad to meet you. _____

    B: It is nice to meet you, too. _____

7. A: My boyfriend is fifty-five years old. _____

    B: But you are only twenty-seven. _____

THE PRESENT NEGATIVE OF *BE*

1 NEGATIVE STATEMENTS WITH *BE*

Look at the picture. Put a check (✓) next to the sentences that are correct. Change the sentences that are wrong.

1. The women are middle-aged. ___The women are not middle-aged.___

2. Two women are with a man. ___✓___

3. The people are in a house. _____

4. A dog is with three people. _____

5. The dog is black. _____

6. The man is young. _____

7. The women are sisters. _____

8. It is night. _____

9. The women are happy. _____

10. I am in the picture. _____

❷ NEGATIVE STATEMENTS WITH *BE*

Correct the sentences and write them below.

1. Dallas is a state.

   Dallas is not a state. It is a city.

2. California is a country.

   _____

3. Russia is small.

   _____

4. Egypt and China are people.

   _____

5. Boston and New York are in Canada.

   _____

6. Florida is a city.

   _____

7. The sun is cold.

   _____

8. Toyotas and Fords are airplanes.

   _____

9. Ottawa is the capital of the United States.

   _____

10. Cigarettes are good for people.

    _____

11. The sun and the moon are near Earth.

    _____

③ AFFIRMATIVE AND NEGATIVE STATEMENTS WITH *BE*

Complete the sentences. Use **is**, **is not**, **are**, *or* **are not**.

1. Apples _____are not_____ black.

2. The Earth _____ round.

3. The sun _____ cold.

4. Ice cream and chocolate _____ good for you.

5. Lemons _____ yellow.

6. Cars _____ cheap.

7. Peter _____ a name.

8. An elephant _____ a small animal.

9. English, Spanish, and Arabic _____ languages.

10. The president of the United States _____ a doctor.

④ CONTRACTIONS OF AFFIRMATIVE AND NEGATIVE STATEMENTS WITH *BE*

Write the conversations in full form.

1. **A:** Carol's angry with her father. ___Carol is angry with her father.___

   B: I'm not surprised. ___I am not surprised.___

2. **A:** I'm right. _____

   B: No, you aren't. You're wrong. _____

3. **A:** Mrs. Morris isn't well. _____

   B: I know. Her daughter's worried about her. _____

4. **A:** It's time for bed. _____

   B: But I'm not tired. _____

5. **A:** They're my books. _____

   B: No, they're not. They're my books. _____

(continued on next page)

6. A: My keys aren't here. _____

    B: They're in my bag. _____

7. A: Maria and Ali aren't in class today. _____

    B: They're lucky. _____

---

5 **CONTRACTIONS OF AFFIRMATIVE AND NEGATIVE STATEMENTS WITH *BE***

Write the conversations with contractions.

1. A: Carol is angry with her father.   Carol's angry with her father. _____

    B: I am not surprised.   I'm not surprised. _____

2. A: I am afraid. _____

    B: Why? The dog is not dangerous. _____

3. A: The taxi is here. _____

    B: But I am not ready. _____

4. A: You are not from the hospital. _____

    B: No, we are police officers. _____

5. A: They are not bad children. _____

    B: No, but they are bad students. _____

6. A: Your bag is on the table. _____

    B: It is not my bag. _____

7. A: This gift is for you. _____

    B: But it is not my birthday. _____

THE PRESENT OF *BE*: YES / NO QUESTIONS

1 AFFIRMATIVE STATEMENTS AND YES / NO QUESTIONS WITH *BE*

Put a question mark (?) at the end of each question. Put a period (.) at the end of each sentence.

1. Milt Costa is a detective**.**

2. Is Milt Costa a detective**?**

3. Are you Rocky

4. Are you and your classmates worried

5. Is your teacher in school today

6. We are very good students

7. I am very thirsty

8. Is the dog hungry

9. Oregon is near Canada

10. Are the children afraid of the dog

11. Is your car red

12. This exercise is easy

2 YES / NO QUESTIONS AND SHORT ANSWERS WITH *BE*

Match the questions and answers.

1. __d__ Is Preeda from Thailand?
2. ____ Are Pat and Tom American?
3. ____ Are you Lucy Simone?
4. ____ Are you ready?
5. ____ Is the doctor in the office?
6. ____ Are Mr. and Mrs. Saris here?
7. ____ Is the TV in the living room?
8. ____ Is John married?
9. ____ Is the book good?
10. ____ Are you students at King High School?
11. ____ Is your mother home?
12. ____ Are you and the other students happy in this class?

a. Yes, she is. She's in the kitchen with my father.
b. Yes, we are. Our teacher's wonderful.
c. Yes, they're in the garden.
d. Yes, he is. He's from Bangkok.
e. No, we're students at Kennedy High School.
f. No, they're not. They're British.
g. No, it isn't. It's in the bedroom.
h. No, I'm Anna Sanchez.
i. Yes, it is. It's very interesting.
j. No, I'm not. Please wait a minute.
k. Yes, he is. His wife's a detective.
l. Yes, she's with a patient.

3 YES / NO QUESTIONS AND SHORT ANSWERS WITH *BE*

Write questions. Then answer them. Use short answers.

1. Milt Costa / you / are

   ___Are you Milt Costa?___   ___No, I'm not.___

2. you / are / happy

   _____   _____

3. a student / your mother / is

   _____   _____

4. clean / is / your bedroom

   _____   _____

5. are / from Texas / your friends

   _____   _____

6. Carol Winston / your friend / is

   _____   _____

7. a detective / are / you

_____   _____

8. your teacher / is / friendly

_____   _____

9. your mother and father / Canadian / are

_____   _____

10. are / in love / you

_____   _____

11. middle-aged / your classmates / are

_____   _____

THE PAST TENSE OF *BE*; PAST TIME MARKERS

1 AFFIRMATIVE STATEMENTS WITH THE PAST TENSE OF *BE*

Pants $45.00

Jacket $79.99

Shirt $29.99

Tie $16.00

Socks $8.00

Sweater $39.00

Coat $145.00

Pajamas $19.99

Shorts $14.99

Hat $25.00

Gloves $22.00

Shoes $65.00

Kim went shopping at Miller's Department Store. Write sentences about her purchases.
Use **was** *or* **were**.

1.   The pants were $45.

2.   The jacket was $79.99.

3. _____

4. _____

5. _____

6. _____

7. _____

8. _____

9. _____

10. _____

11. _____

12. _____

2   AFFIRMATIVE AND NEGATIVE STATEMENTS WITH THE PAST TENSE OF *BE*

Write sentences. Use **was**, **wasn't**, **were**, *or* **weren't**.

1. Abraham Lincoln / born / in England

     Abraham Lincoln wasn't born in England.

2. Picasso and Michelangelo / painters

     Picasso and Michelangelo were painters.

3. William Shakespeare and Charles Dickens / Canadian

   _____

4. Bill Clinton / the first president of the United States

   _____

(continued on next page)

5. Charlie Chaplin and Marilyn Monroe / movie stars

_____

6. The end of World War I / in 1942

_____

7. *Titanic* / the name of a movie

_____

8. Toronto and Washington, D.C. / big cities 300 years ago

_____

9. Indira Gandhi and Napoleon / famous people

_____

10. Nelson Mandela / a political leader

_____

11. Oregon and Hawaii / part of the United States / in 1776

_____

12. Disneyland / a famous place / 100 years ago

_____

3 YES / NO QUESTIONS AND SHORT ANSWERS WITH THE PAST TENSE OF *BE*

Find and correct the mistake in each question. Then answer the questions. Use short answers.

Was
1. ~~Were~~ your mother at home last night? ___Yes, she was. (OR: No, she wasn't.)___

2. You were a student ten years ago? _____

3. Are you in English class yesterday? _____

4. Was all the students in class last week? _____

5. Is the weather nice yesterday? _____

6. Your teacher was at work two days ago? _____

❹ THE PRESENT AND PAST OF *BE*

Complete the conversation. Use **is**, **are**, **was**, *or* **were**.

A: It _____is_____ a beautiful day.
        1.

B: Yes, it is—especially because the weather _____was_____ so terrible yesterday. The
                                                        2.
weather in this city _____ so strange. One day it _____ warm, and
                             3.   **4.**
the next day it _____ cold.
                      5.

A: You _____ right about that. In my country, it _____ always warm
              6.   **7.**
and sunny.

B: _____ it warm in the winter, too?
        8.

A: Uh-huh. It _____ usually between 70 and 90 degrees. Last Christmas I
                       9.
_____ home for two weeks, and it _____ sunny and warm. My
      10.   **11.**
friends and I _____ at the beach every day. How about you? _____
                    12.   **13.**
you here this past Christmas?

B: Yeah. My parents _____ here for five days for a visit. We _____
                              14.   **15.**
cold most of the time, and my mother _____ ill for a few days. They
                                              16.
_____ happy to see me, but they _____ glad to leave this awful
      17.   **18.**
weather.

A: _____ your parents back home now?
        19.

B: No, they _____ on another vacation—this time, in a warm place.
                      20.

UNIT

5 COUNT NOUNS; A / AN

1 NOUNS

Match the people with their occupations.

1. __d__ Romario   **a.** actor
2. ____ Tom Cruise   **b.** ice skater
3. ____ Elizabeth II   **c.** musician
4. ____ Céline Dion   **d.** soccer player
5. ____ Neil Armstrong   **e.** queen
6. ____ Yo Yo Ma   **f.** astronaut
7. ____ Kristi Yamaguchi   **g.** actress
8. ____ Sharon Stone   **h.** singer

2 NOUNS WITH *A / AN*

Write sentences about the people in Exercise 1.

1.   Romario is a soccer player. _____

2. _____

3. _____

4. _____

5. _____

6. _____

7. _____

8. _____

3 PLURAL NOUNS

Say these plural nouns. Then write them in the correct columns.

			/ z /	/ ɪz /	/ s /
~~actresses~~	dictionaries	roommates	boys	actresses	carrots
boxes	girls	sons			
~~boys~~	houses	states			
~~carrots~~	lemons	students			
classes	notebooks	watches			

4 PLURAL NOUNS

Complete the sentences. Use the plural form of the words in the box.

actress	country	river	university
~~car~~	man	song	watch
city	mountain	state	~~woman~~
continent	province		

1. Toyotas and Fords are _____cars_____.

2. Mrs. Robb and Ms. Hernandez are _____women_____.

3. Mr. Katz and John Mallin are _____.

4. "A Hard Day's Night" and "Happy Birthday to You" are _____.

5. London and Cairo are _____.

6. The Nile and the Amazon are _____.

7. Asia and Africa are _____.

8. Florida and Michigan are _____.

9. Brazil and Kenya are _____.

10. Ontario and Quebec are _____.

11. Harvard and Yale are _____.

12. Seikos and Rolexes are _____.

13. Demi Moore and Julia Roberts are _____.

14. The Himalayas and the Alps are _____.

5 IRREGULAR PLURAL NOUNS

Write the singular or plural form of the nouns.

1. 4 women
+ 1 __woman__
 5 __women__

2. 1 child
+ 2 _____
 3 _____

3. 1 tooth
+ 6 _____
 7 _____

4. 3 feet
+ 1 _____
 4 _____

5. 6 grandchildren
+ 1 _____
 7 _____

6. 8 people
+ 1 _____
 9 _____

7. 1 sister-in-law
+ 2 _____
 3 _____

6 SINGULAR AND PLURAL NOUNS

*Unscramble the words. Then write sentences with **it's** or **they're**. Add **a** or **an** where necessary.*

1. enp __pen__   __It's a pen.__

2. latseb __tables__   __They're tables.__

3. racs _____   _____

4. usheo _____   _____

5. kobos _____   _____

6. arseer _____   _____

7. seey _____   _____

8. esxbo _____   _____

9. veno _____   _____

10. geg _____   _____

11. ogsd _____   _____

12. chatw _____   _____

DESCRIPTIVE ADJECTIVES

① OPPOSITES OF ADJECTIVES

Write the opposites of the underlined words.

1. **A:** Is the man <u>tall</u>?

   B: Yes, but his sons are _____ short _____.

2. **A:** Is your dog <u>small</u>?

   B: Yes, but the other dogs are _____.

3. **A:** Is the book <u>interesting</u>?

   B: Yes, but the movie is _____.

4. **A:** Is Ann <u>thin</u>?

   B: Yes, but her daughter is _____.

5. **A:** Is this watch <u>cheap</u>?

   B: Yes, but that watch is _____.

6. **A:** Is your room <u>clean</u>?

   B: Yes, but the other rooms are _____.

7. **A:** Is the little girl <u>quiet</u>?

   B: Yes, but the little boys are _____.

8. **A:** Are the apples <u>good</u>?

   B: Yes, but the bananas are _____.

9. **A:** Are your shoes <u>old</u>? _____.

   B: Yes, but my shirt is _____.

10. **A:** Are your feet <u>hot</u>?

    B: Yes, but my hands are _____.

2 ADJECTIVES AND NOUNS

Find the mistakes. Then write correct sentences.

1. The olds shoes are over there.

   The old shoes are over there.

2. They are men honest.

_____

3. They are talls girls.

_____

4. They are animals intelligent.

_____

5. Those books are expensives.

_____

6. Eggs are whites or browns.

_____

7. They are actors good.

_____

8. These watches are cheaps.

_____

9. They are stories interesting.

_____

3 ADJECTIVES AND NOUNS

Combine each two sentences into one sentence.

1. You are boys. You are bad.

   You are bad boys.

2. It is a book. It is great.

_____

3. Bill Clinton is a politican. Bill Clinton is famous.

_____

4. She is a singer. She is beautiful.

_____

5. They are students. They are intelligent.

_____

6. He is a man. He is interesting.

_____

7. It is a camera. It is expensive.

_____

8. It is a story. It is long.

_____

9. We are doctors. We are good.

_____

10. You are a woman. You are lucky.

_____

PREPOSITIONS OF PLACE

1 PREPOSITIONS OF PLACE

Draw a picture of each sentence.

1. A cat is under a chair.

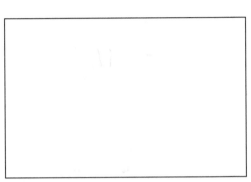

2. A dog is on a chair.

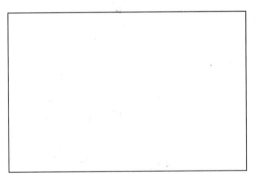

3. A ball is between a dog and a cat.

4. A man is next to a chair.

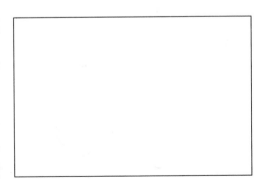

5. An apple is next to a banana.

6. A woman is behind a little girl.

7. A ball is under a car.

8. A bicycle is next to a house.

9. Some flowers are between two trees.

10. Two boxes are on a bed.

2 PREPOSITIONS OF PLACE

*Look at the map on page A-2 of your Student Book. Complete the sentences. Use **near**, **between**, **next to**, or **in**.*

1. Seattle is _____ in _____ Washington.

2. Saskatchewan is _____ Manitoba and Alberta.

3. Pennsylvania is _____ New Jersey.

4. Maine is _____ Massachusetts.

5. Halifax is _____ Nova Scotia.

6. Kansas is _____ Arkansas and Iowa.

7. Indiana is _____ Ohio and Illinois.

8. Prince Edward Island is _____ Canada.

9. Idaho is _____ Oregon.

10. Ottawa is _____ Montreal.

8 PRESENT PROGRESSIVE

1 AFFIRMATIVE STATEMENTS WITH THE PRESENT PROGRESSIVE

Match the sentences.

1. __d__ Lou's at the supermarket.
2. ____ Paul's at the bank.
3. ____ Linda's in the library.
4. ____ The football players are on the field.
5. ____ The doctor's at the hospital.
6. ____ Doug's at the shopping mall.
7. ____ Susan's in the bathroom.
8. ____ Mrs. Thompson and her family are in the dining room.
9. ____ Sharon and her boyfriend are at the beach.
10. ____ Pete's at the office.

a. They're playing football.
b. She's studying.
c. She's examining a patient.
d. He's buying groceries.
e. He's getting some money.
f. They're eating dinner.
g. She's taking a shower.
h. They're lying in the sun.
i. He's writing a report.
j. He's buying a shirt.

2 BASE FORM AND VERB + -ING

Write the missing form of each verb.

Base Form	Base Form + -ing
1. have	having
2. sit	sitting
3. get	_____
4. shine	_____
5. _____	raining
6. _____	making
7. watch	_____

	Base Form	**Base Form + -ing**
8.	listen	_____
9.	_____	running
10.	hit	_____
11.	_____	talking
12.	drive	_____
13.	do	_____
14.	_____	putting
15.	_____	beginning
16.	study	_____

3 AFFIRMATIVE AND NEGATIVE STATEMENTS WITH THE PRESENT PROGRESSIVE

Write true sentences.

1. I / do / a grammar exercise

   I am doing a grammar exercise.

2. I / sleep

   I am not sleeping.

3. I / have / a good time

4. The sun / shine

5. It / rain

6. It / get / dark

7. I / listen / to the radio

(continued on next page)

8. I / talk / on the phone

_____

9. I / sit / on a chair

_____

10. My best friend / sit / next to me

_____

11. My neighbors / make / a lot of noise

_____

12. I / write / with a pencil

_____

4 SUBJECT VERB AGREEMENT WITH THE PRESENT PROGRESSIVE

Complete the postcard. Use the correct form of the verbs in parentheses.

January 11

Greetings from Vermont from all of us. We ____are having____ a great
                                            1. (have)
time. It _____ a little right now, and it is cold. Many people
         2. (snow)
_____, but we are too tired. We _____ at the
   3. (ski)   **4. (relax)**
moment. Ellen and I _____ in the coffee shop. She
                        5. (sit)
_____ and I _____ to you! The girls
   6. (read)   **7. (write)**
_____ a snowman outside. They _____
   8. (make)   **9. (enjoy)**
themselves a lot. Naturally, Tommy _____ a video game!
                                      10. (play)
We hope you are well.

Love from all of us,

Nick

5 YES / NO QUESTIONS WITH THE PRESENT PROGRESSIVE

*Write questions. Then answer them. Use short answers. If you don't
know an answer, write* **I don't know**.

1. doing / you / a grammar exercise / are

    Are you doing a grammar exercise?   Yes, I am.

2. glasses / wearing / you / are

    _____   _____

3. your English teacher / correcting / is / papers

    _____   _____

4. TV / you and a friend / watching / are

    _____   _____

5. your classmates / doing / this exercise / now / are

    _____   _____

6. are / having / with your neighbors / dinner

    _____   _____

7. shining / the sun / is

    _____   _____

8. your friends / are / for you / waiting

    _____   _____

9. working / are / your parents

    _____   _____

10. ice cream / eating / are / you

    _____   _____

11. is / helping / your teacher / you

    _____   _____

12. outside / children / are / playing

    _____   _____

6 YES / NO QUESTIONS WITH THE PRESENT PROGRESSIVE

Write questions. Use the words in parentheses.

1. **A:** Yoko's in class.

   B: ___Is she listening to the teacher?_____ (listen to the teacher)

   A: Probably.

2. **A:** Mary's in the bedroom.

   B: _____ (sleep)

   A: Maybe.

3. **A:** All the children are at the playground.

   B: _____ (play)

   A: Probably.

4. **A:** My son and his friend are at the swimming pool.

   B: _____ (swim)

   A: I think so.

5. **A:** John's in the post office.

   B: _____ (buy stamps)

   A: Probably.

6. **A:** My parents are on vacation.

   B: _____ (have a good time)

   A: I hope so.

7. **A:** Carol's at the hospital.

   B: _____ (visit someone)

   A: I don't know.

8. **A:** Warren and Anne are outside.

   B: _____ (play tennis)

   A: I think so.

9. A: Julie's under the car.

   B: _____ (fix something)

   A: Maybe.

10. A: Michael isn't here yet.

   B: _____ (come)

   A: I think so.

11. A: There are two people in the hall.

   B: _____ (wait for me)

   A: I don't know.

12. A: A man's behind you.

   B: _____ (follow me)

   A: I don't know.

UNIT

QUESTIONS WITH *WHO, WHAT,* AND *WHERE*

1 QUESTION WORDS

Write the correct question words. Use **who**, **what**, *or* **where**.

1. __Who__?	**a.**	My mother.
2. __Where__?	**b.**	At home.
3. _____?	**c.**	My best friend.
4. _____?	**d.**	In Texas.
5. _____?	**e.**	On Park Street.
6. _____?	**f.**	A sandwich.
7. _____?	**g.**	Abraham Lincoln and John F. Kennedy.
8. _____?	**h.**	Brazil.
9. _____?	**i.**	Shakespeare.
10. _____?	**j.**	Soccer and basketball.
11. _____?	**k.**	Under the bed.
12. _____?	**l.**	A bird.

② *WH-* QUESTIONS AND ANSWERS WITH *BE*

Write questions. Then find an answer for each question in Exercise 1.
Write the answers below.

1. were / parents / where / your

    Where were your parents?   At home.

2. in / is / car / the / who

    Who is in the car?   My mother.

3. what / you / good at / sports / are

4. from / where / they / are

5. in / who / your / the / garden / was / woman

6. Dallas / where / is

7. shoes / are / where / my

8. bag / was / the / what / in

9. post office / the / is / where

10. who / your / writer / favorite / is

11. the United States / who / two / presidents / are / famous / of

12. tree / what / the / is / in

❸ QUESTION WORDS

Complete the sentences. Use **who**, **what**, *or* **where**.

NORMA: _____Where_____'s Doug?
                    1.

    DAD: I don't know. _____ time is it?
                                    2.

NORMA: It's 8:30.

    DAD: Maybe he's at the movies. Why? _____'s the problem?
                                                        3.

NORMA: There's a phone call for him.

    DAD: _____'s on the phone?
                        4.

NORMA: A girl.

    DAD: _____'s her name?
                        5.

NORMA: Minjung.

    DAD: _____'s Minjung?
                        6.

NORMA: Doug's girlfriend.

    DAD: Doug's girlfriend?

NORMA: Uh-huh.

    DAD: Minjung's an unusual name. _____'s she from?
                                            7.

NORMA: Dad, I don't know. She's not my girlfriend.

❹ *WH-* QUESTIONS

Write the questions. Use **who**, **what**, *or* **where**.

  1. A: _____Who is he? (OR: Who's he?)_____

    B: He's one of the students in my English class.

  2. A: _____

    B: The hospital? It's on Porter Street.

  3. A: _____

    B: John Wayne? He was an actor.

  4. A: _____

    B: Room 203 . . . Room 203. I'm sorry. I don't know.

5. A: _____

   B: I think your keys are on the TV.

6. A: _____

   B: King Hussein and François Mitterand were leaders of their countries.

7. A: _____

   B: On the phone? It was a friend from school.

8. A: _____

   B: Cadillacs are cars.

9. A: _____

   B: It's my answering machine.

10. A: _____

   B: The wastepaper basket is next to the desk.

11. A: _____

   B: Last night? I was at home.

10 POSSESSIVE NOUNS AND POSSESSIVE ADJECTIVES; QUESTIONS WITH *WHOSE*

① POSSESSIVE ADJECTIVES

Match the questions and answers.

1. __c__ Is John your son?
2. ____ Is your home on this street?
3. ____ Is he Joe and Karen's son?
4. ____ Is Ms. Turner's home near here?
5. ____ Is she a famous actress?
6. ____ Are they rich?
7. ____ Is Mr. Wong a doctor?
8. ____ Is that man your friend?
9. ____ Is our table ready?

a. No, their son is in another state.
b. No, but her office is.
c. No, Mark is my son.
d. No, it isn't. Please wait a minute.
e. No, we are visiting here.
f. No, her sister is.
g. Yes, his office is near the hospital.
h. Yes, his name is Sam Miller.
i. No, but their friends are.

② POSSESSIVE ADJECTIVES

Complete the conversations. Use **my**, **your**, **his**, **her**, **our**, *or* **their**.

1.   **JACK:** Is that my car?

   JILL: No, _____your_____ car isn't here.

2.   **BOB:** Jim, is this _____ bag?

   JIM: No, it isn't. Maybe it's Sue and Harry's bag.

   BOB: No, _____ bag is over there.

3. **MR. WOLF:** Is this Mrs. Waller's box?

   BARBARA: No, that's not _____ box.

   MR. WOLF: Is it Mr. Luca's box?

   BARBARA: Maybe it's _____ box. I'm not sure.

4. **Mrs. Yu:** Is this your family's dog?

  Ben: No, _____ dog is black.

  Mrs. Yu: Is it Mr. and Mrs. Haley's dog?

  Ben: No, _____ dog is white.

5. **Alan:** Is this your office?

  Ron: No, _____ office is on the second floor.

  Alan: Is it Norma's office?

  Ron: No, _____ office is on the first floor.

6. **Becky:** Stella, is that _____ husband with you in the picture?

  Stella: Yes, _____ name is Dave.

  Becky: And who's this?

  Stella: It's _____ daughter. _____ name is Marie.

3 POSSESSIVE ADJECTIVES AND SUBJECT PRONOUNS

Complete the sentences. Use subject pronouns or possessive adjectives.

1. Hi. I'm Yoko. _____I_____'m from Japan. _____My_____ home is in Tokyo.

2. This is Doug. _____'s in New York. _____ bedroom is always messy.

3. This is Carol. _____'s in Oregon. Yoko is _____ roommate.

4. This is Pete, and this is Elenore. _____'re married. _____ last name is Winston. This is _____ home. _____'s beautiful.

5. Hello. I'm Bertha and this is Lulu. _____'re friends. _____ homes are in Florida.

6. Hi. I'm Norma. _____'m not married, but _____ boyfriend is very handsome.

7. This is Milt Costa. _____'s a detective. _____ office is on Ridgewood Street.

(continued on next page)

8. My husband and I are happy to meet you. _____'re here on vacation.

   _____ hotel is near the beach. _____ name is the Grand Hotel.

   _____'s a very nice place.

9. These are our children. _____ names are Katie and Chris. _____'re

   not at home this month. _____'re with my mother.

---

4 POSSESSIVE NOUNS, POSSESSIVE ADJECTIVES, AND SUBJECT PRONOUNS

Rewrite the sentences. Change the underlined words.

1. <u>Pete Winston's</u> a businessman.

   He's a businessman.

2. <u>Pete Winston's</u> wife's a writer.

   His wife's a writer.

3. <u>Pedro's</u> last name is Barba.

   _____

4. <u>Pedro's</u> a grandfather.

   _____

5. <u>His granddaughters'</u> names are Lydia and Daphne.

   _____

6. <u>Lydia's</u> twelve years old.

   _____

7. <u>Lydia's</u> hair is long.

   _____

8. <u>Pedro's</u> dogs are always outside.

   _____

9. <u>Daphne's</u> eyes are blue.

   _____

10. <u>Daphne's</u> afraid of the dogs.

    _____

11. <u>The girls</u> were with their grandfather yesterday.

_____

12. <u>Pedro</u> was with his dogs.

_____

13. <u>The dogs'</u> food was in the garage.

_____

14. <u>The dogs</u> were in the garage.

_____

15. <u>The children's</u> friends were not with them yesterday.

_____

16. <u>The children</u> were happy to be with their grandfather.

_____

5 QUESTIONS WITH *WHOSE*

*Larry is at the supermarket. He has the wrong bag of food. Write
questions. Use* **whose**.

(continued on next page)

1. This is not my coffee.

   Whose coffee is this?

2. These are not my apples.

   Whose apples are these?

3. These are not my eggs.

   _____

4. These are not my bananas.

   _____

5. This is not my bread.

   _____

6. These are not my potatoes.

   _____

7. This is not my cake.

   _____

8. This is not my milk.

   _____

9. This is not my orange juice.

   _____

10. These are not my potato chips.

    _____

11. These are not my carrots.

    _____

12. This is not my bag.

    _____

6 POSSESSIVE NOUNS

Correct the sentences. Add ' or 's where necessary.

1. **A:** Is this Steve's report?

   B: I don't think so.

2. **A:** What are your daughters' names?

   B: Norma and Carol.

3. **A:** What's Ms. Winston first name?

   B: It's Elenore.

4. **A:** Where's the men room?

   B: It's over there.

5. **A:** Is that your husband brother?

   B: No, that's my brother.

6. **A:** Where are the babies mothers?

   B: In the other room.

7. **A:** Is your school for girls and boys?

   B: No, it's a girls school.

8. **A:** Are your brothers wives friendly?

   B: One is.

9. **A:** Is that your son car?

   B: No, it isn't.

10. **A:** Where's the doctor office?

    B: It's on Cambridge Avenue.

11. **A:** A teacher job is difficult.

    B: I know.

12. **A:** I can't find my teacher.

    B: Look in the teachers lunchroom. Many teachers are in there.

7 POSSESSIVE NOUNS

Complete the sentences.

1. The wallet is ___Al Green's___.

2. The handbag is _____.

3. The car is _____.

4. The sweatshirt is _____.

5. The notebook is _____.

6. The jeans are _____.

7. The desk is _____.

8. The composition is _____.

9. The shoes are _____.

QUESTIONS WITH *WHEN* AND *WHAT* + NOUN; PREPOSITIONS; ORDINAL NUMBERS

 PREPOSITIONS OF TIME

Write the words in the correct columns.

~~4:00~~	May	the morning
January 15, 2000	~~Wednesday~~	the spring
night	Thursday	~~December~~
the evening	half past six	1888
June 30th	December 3rd	the summer

AT	IN	ON
4:00	December	Wednesday

❷ PREPOSITIONS OF TIME

*Michael doesn't have his appointment book. It's at your house. He telephones you on September 24. Look at his appointment book and answer his questions. Use **at**, **in**, or **on**.*

Wed. Sept. 24

2:30   meeting with director

Thurs. Sept. 25

9 A.M.   doctor's appt.

3 P.M.   job interview

8 P.M.   concert

Fri. Sept. 26

8:30   piano lesson

lunch with Nancy Morrison

Eve.   baseball game

Sat. Sept. 27

Scott's birthday

P.M.   Tennis with Henry (after lunch)

1. When is my piano lesson on Friday morning?

_____It's at 8:30._____

2. What time this afternoon is my appointment with the director?

_____

3. And when is my doctor's appointment tomorrow?

_____

4. When's my lunch with Nancy Morrison?

_____

5. I know Scott's birthday is this week, but when is it?

_____

6. What time is the concert tomorrow?

_____

7. I know I have a tennis game with Henry on Saturday. Is it in the morning?

_____

8. What about my job interview tomorrow? When's that?

_____

9. When is the baseball game on Friday? In the afternoon?

_____

❸ *WH-* QUESTIONS

Laura is always confused. Write questions.

1. A: Is lunch at two o'clock?
   B: No, it isn't.
   A: Then _____what time is lunch?_____
   B: It's at twelve o'clock.

2. A: Is today Monday?
   B: No, it isn't.
   A: Then _____what day is it?_____
   B: It's Sunday.

3. A: Is today June 10th?
   B: No, it isn't.
   A: Then _____
   B: It's June 11th.

4. A: Is it 10:30?
   B: No, it isn't.
   A: Then _____
   B: It's 11:30.

(continued on next page)

5. **A:** Is the meeting today?
   B: No, it isn't.
   A: Then _____
   B: It's tomorrow.

6. **A:** Is the meeting in the afternoon?
   B: No, it isn't.
   A: Then _____
   B: It's in the evening.

7. **A:** The meeting's at six o'clock, isn't it?
   B: No, it isn't.
   A: Then _____
   B: It's at 7:30.

8. **A:** I need some money. Is the bank open on Saturday?
   B: No, it isn't.
   A: Then _____
   B: It's open Monday, Tuesday, Wednesday, Thursday, and Friday.

9. **A:** Is today your birthday?
   B: No, it isn't.
   A: Then _____
   B: It's tomorrow.

4 ORDINAL NUMBERS

Write the numbers.

1. sixth _____6th_____
2. forty-fourth _____44th_____
3. ninth _____
4. twelfth _____
5. twenty-third _____
6. fifty-first _____

7. seventy-second _____
8. eightieth _____
9. ninety-fifth _____
10. one hundred and first _____
11. one hundred and sixteenth _____
12. two hundredth _____

5 ORDINAL NUMBERS

Write the words for the numbers.

1. 4th ___fourth___

2. 38th ___thirty-eighth___

3. 3rd _____

4. 11th _____

5. 15th _____

6. 20th _____

7. 31st _____

8. 47th _____

9. 66th _____

10. 82nd _____

11. 99th _____

12. 103rd _____

6 ORDINAL NUMBERS

Write the street names.

1. ___Third Avenue and Thirty-second Street___

2. _____

3. _____

4. _____

5. _____

6. _____

7. _____

1.

2. 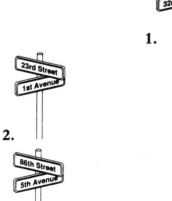 **3.**  **4.**

5. **6.** **7.**

7 ORDINAL NUMBERS AND PREPOSITIONS OF TIME

When are the birthdays of Carol's friends and relatives? Write the dates.

JANUARY

S	M	T	W	T	F	S
				1 Dan	2	3 Ellen
4	5	6	7	8	9	10 Aunt Valerie
11	12	13	14	15	16	17
18	19	20 Yoko	21	22	23	24
25	26	27	28	29	30	31 Norma

FEBRUARY

S	M	T	W	T	F	S
1	2 Mom	3	4	5 Uncle Bob	6	7
8	9 Grandma	10	11	12	13	14
15	16	17	18 Doug	19	20	21
22 Bertha	23	24	25	26	27	28

1. When is her mother's birthday? _It's on February second._
2. When is Norma's birthday? _____
3. When is Aunt Valerie's birthday? _____
4. When is Uncle Bob's birthday? _____
5. When is Yoko's birthday? _____
6. When is her grandmother's birthday? _____
7. When is Ellen's birthday? _____
8. When is Doug's birthday? _____
9. When is Dan's birthday? _____
10. When is Bertha's birthday? _____

QUESTIONS WITH *WHO, WHOM,* AND *WHY; WH-* QUESTIONS AND THE PRESENT PROGRESSIVE

1 *WH-* QUESTIONS WITH THE PRESENT PROGRESSIVE

Look at the picture and answer the questions.

1. What is Doug buying? <u>A pineapple.</u>

2. What is the storekeeper weighing? _____

3. Why are the people standing in line? _____

4. Who is wearing a black dress? _____

5. Where are the people standing? _____

6. What is the young woman wearing? _____

7. Where is the young woman standing? _____

2 *WH-* QUESTIONS AND ANSWERS WITH THE PRESENT PROGRESSIVE

Write questions.

1. leaving / are / why / you / so early

   <u>Why are you leaving so early?</u>

2. the gift / where / you / are / hiding

   _____

3. is / on the door / who / knocking

   _____

4. your / are / what / children / wearing

   _____

5. waiting for / she / who / is

   _____

6. you / looking for / what / are

   _____

7. they / are / why / shouting

   _____

8. are / where / they / going

   _____

9. is / sending / him / why / a gift / she

   _____

10. doing / you / what / are

    _____

❸ WH- QUESTIONS WITH THE PRESENT PROGRESSIVE

Write the correct questions from Exercise 2.

1.   Why are they shouting? _____

They are excited.

2. _____

I'm fixing the lamp.

3. _____

I'm bored.

4. _____

My keys.

5. _____

Under the bed.

6. _____

I think it's the mailman.

7. _____

T-shirts and blue jeans.

8. _____

Her boyfriend.

9. _____

To the doctor.

10. _____

It's his birthday.

4 *WHO* FOR SUBJECT OR OBJECT

Complete the conversations. Circle the correct answers and write them on the lines.

1. **A:** What are you doing?

   B: I'm talking on the phone.

   A: Who _____ are you talking _____ to?

        a. is talking   **(b.)** are you talking

   B: A friend.

2. **A:** What are you doing?

   B: I'm cooking for the party.

   A: Who _____ to the party?

        a. is coming   **b.** are they coming

   B: Some people from work.

3. **A:** Where's Kevin?

   B: He's playing in the backyard.

   A: Who _____ with?

        a. is playing   **b.** is he playing

   B: Some friends from school.

4. **A:** The music is nice.

   B: Yes, it is.

   A: Who _____?

        a. is playing   **b.** is he playing

   B: My son.

5. **A:** What are you doing?

   B: I'm writing a letter.

   A: Who _____?

        a. is writing   **b.** are you writing to

   B: My cousin.

6. A: Are the kids at home?

   B: No, they're helping someone with some packages.

   A: Who _____?

      a. is helping   **b.** are they helping

   B: The older couple down the street.

7. A: Nurse Richards, is anybody still waiting in the office?

   B: Yes.

   A: Who _____?

      a. is waiting   **b.** are they waiting

   B: Ms. Gomez and Mr. Robertson.

5 WH- QUESTIONS

Write questions.

1. A: Doug is painting something.

   B: _What is he painting?_

   A: I'm not sure. I think it's a portrait.

2. A: I'm reading.

   B: _____

   A: The newspaper.

3. A: The kids are eating.

   B: _____

   A: Some ice cream.

4. A: My husband's cooking.

   B: _____

   A: Dinner.

5. A: Someone's coming.

   B: _____

   A: I think it's your sister.

(continued on next page)

6. A: I'm going to bed.

    B: _____

    A: I'm tired.

7. A: We're going.

    B: _____

    A: To the supermarket.

8. A: I'm selling my car.

    B: _____

    A: It's old.

9. A: Monica and Chris are swimming.

    B: _____

    A: In the pool near the park.

10. A: I'm watching TV.

    B: _____

    A: A baseball game.

11. A: The police officers are watching someone.

    B: _____

    A: That young man over there.

12. A: Jane's dating someone new.

    B: _____

    A: Eric Snyder.

SIMPLE PRESENT TENSE: AFFIRMATIVE AND NEGATIVE STATEMENTS

1 AFFIRMATIVE STATEMENTS WITH THE SIMPLE PRESENT TENSE

Read the job description. Answer the questions. Use the words in the box.

cook	flight attendant	pilot	salesperson
doctor	~~mechanic~~	professor	secretary

1. Daniel fixes cars. He works in a garage. What is he?

   He's a mechanic.

2. Dina and Lesley answer telephones and type letters. They work in a college office. What are they?

   _____

3. Captain Phillips goes to the airport every day. He flies airplanes. What is he?

   _____

4. Kay Williams gives lectures and meets with students. She works in a university. What is she?

   _____

5. Ben and Rachel work on an airplane. They serve meals and drinks to passengers. What are they?

   _____

6. I work in a restaurant. I prepare the food. What am I?

   _____

(continued on next page)

7. I work in a store. I sell refrigerators. What am I?

_____

8. Ellen helps sick people. She works in a hospital. What is she?

_____

② AFFIRMATIVE AND NEGATIVE STATEMENTS WITH THE SIMPLE PRESENT TENSE

Complete each sentence with the correct verb. Use the simple present tense.

1. Mary is a taxi driver. She _____drives_____ a taxi.

2. Stuart is a Spanish teacher. He _____ Spanish.

3. Maria Domingo is a singer. She _____.

4. Nassos Morona is a dancer. He _____.

5. Bill Bright is a baseball player. He _____ baseball.

6. Shirley Simpson is a bank manager. She _____ a bank.

7. Sam and Victor are trash collectors. They _____ trash.

8. Margaret and Phil are house painters. They _____ houses.

9. Lou is a window washer. He _____ windows.

10. Oscar, Tom, and Steve are firefighters. They _____ fires.

③ NEGATIVE STATEMENTS WITH THE SIMPLE PRESENT TENSE

*Complete the sentences. Use **don't** or **doesn't**.*

1. Doug lives in New York, but Carol _____doesn't_____.

2. Carol lives in Oregon, but her parents _____don't_____.

3. Carol has a roommate, but Doug _____.

4. Doug has green eyes, but Norma _____.

5. Elenore and Pete live in New York, but Bertha and Lulu _____.

6. Doug's friend, Norman, has a brother, but Doug _____.

7. Yoko studies hard, but Carol and Doug _____.

8. Carol likes her way of life at college, but Pete and Elenore _____.

9. Some students think English grammar is easy, but I _____.

10. My teacher likes this grammar exercise, but my classmates and I _____.

4 AFFIRMATIVE AND NEGATIVE STATEMENTS WITH THE SIMPLE PRESENT TENSE

Complete the conversation. Use the correct form of the verbs in parentheses.

A: Tell me about you and your family.

B: My husband and I _____*are*_____ pretty traditional. I _____ care of the
          1. (be)   2. (take)

  home, and he _____ to work. He _____ a business in town, but we
               3. (go)   4. (have)

  _____ in an old house in the country.
      5. (live)

A: Alone?

B: Oh, no. We _____ alone. We _____ eight children—seven boys and
           6. (not live)   7. (have)

  one girl. Two of them _____ with us anymore. Our daughter _____
               8. (not live)   9. (be)

  married, and she _____ with her family. She _____ two children.
            10. (live)   11. (have)

  One of our sons _____ also married, but he _____ any children.
            12. (be)   13. (not have)

  Our other six sons _____ with us. One of them, Marvin, _____ at
            14. (live)   15. (study)

  the local college and _____ part-time. He _____ home every
            16. (work)   17. (leave)

  morning at around six o'clock and _____ home until seven or eight in the
               18. (not come)

  evening. It _____ a good schedule at all. Our son Russell _____
          19. (not be)   20. (help)

  my husband, and the other boys _____ to high school.
                  21. (go)

A: Are you busy all the time?

B: Oh, yes. I _____ much free time at all. That's why we _____ to rest
          22. (not have)   23. (try)

  on Sundays. We _____ up until nine o'clock.
          24. (not get)

5 AFFIRMATIVE AND NEGATIVE STATEMENTS WITH THE SIMPLE PRESENT TENSE

Correct the sentences. Use words from the box.

a big population	grass	the sun
during the day	mice	0°C
in the east	Antarctic	100°C
a hot climate	sand	big ears

1. The Sun rises in the west.

   The Sun doesn't rise in the west. It rises in the east.

2. Water boils at 90°C.

3. Water freezes at 5°C.

4. The sun goes around the Earth.

5. Penguins come from the Arctic.

6. Cows eat meat.

7. China has a small population.

8. Deserts have a lot of water.

9. Elephants have small ears.

10. Egypt has a cold climate.

11. The sun shines at night.

12. Mice run after cats.

SIMPLE PRESENT TENSE: YES / NO QUESTIONS AND SHORT ANSWERS

1 YES / NO QUESTIONS WITH THE SIMPLE PRESENT TENSE

Write the questions in the correct boxes.

1. Do you feel a pain here?
2. Do you know how to type?
3. Do you want a plastic bag or a paper bag?
4. Do you have any experience?
5. Do you want a one-bedroom or a two-bedroom apartment?
6. Do you get many headaches?
7. Do you have any other fresh fish?
8. Do you speak a foreign language?
9. Do you want a place near the center of town?
10. Does your back hurt?
11. Does this orange juice cost $2.50?
12. Does the house have two bathrooms?

PEOPLE OFTEN ASK THIS AT . . .

A. A JOB INTERVIEW	B. A DOCTOR'S OFFICE
	Do you feel a pain here?
C. A REAL ESTATE OFFICE	**D. A SUPERMARKET**

2 YES / NO QUESTIONS AND SHORT ANSWERS WITH THE SIMPLE PRESENT TENSE

Match the questions and answers.

1. __e__ Does the sun go around the Earth?

2. ____ Do banks have money?

3. ____ Do you speak English perfectly?

4. ____ Does England have many mountains?

5. ____ Do supermarkets sell cars?

6. ____ Does the president of the United States live on the moon?

7. ____ Does the president of the United States live in the White House?

8. ____ Do you eat every day?

a. Yes, it does.

b. No, they don't.

c. No, I don't.

d. Yes, I do.

e. No, it doesn't.

f. Yes, they do.

g. No, he doesn't.

h. Yes, he does.

3 YES / NO QUESTIONS AND SHORT ANSWERS WITH THE SIMPLE PRESENT TENSE

Answer the questions. Use short answers.

	Michael	Mary	Karen	Larry
ROCK MUSIC	✓	X	X	X
CLASSICAL MUSIC	X	✓	X	✓
JAZZ	X	✓	X	✓
COUNTRY MUSIC	X	✓	X	X
FOLK MUSIC	✓	X	X	✓
✓ = YES X = NO				

1. Does Michael like rock music? _____Yes, he does._____

2. Do Karen and Larry like country music? _____No, they don't._____

3. Does Mary like jazz? _____

4. Does Karen like folk music? _____

5. Do Michael and Larry like folk music? _____

6. Does Larry like jazz? _____

7. Does Mary like folk music? _____

8. Does Larry like classical music?   _____

9. Do Karen and Larry like rock music? _____

10. Do Mary and Larry like jazz?   _____

4 YES / NO QUESTIONS WITH THE SIMPLE PRESENT TENSE

Find the mistake in each sentence. Then correct the mistake.

    Do you
1. ~~You~~ need any help?

2. Does your roommate likes your girlfriend?

3. The teacher wear glasses?

4. Do Mr. Flagg have a car?

5. Does Jack and Jill sleep until ten o'clock?

6. Peter eat fast?

7. Are she leave for work at the same time every day?

8. Is the dog eat two times a day?

9. Does the doctor has your telephone number?

10. Football players play in the summer?

5 YES / NO QUESTIONS WITH THE SIMPLE PRESENT TENSE

Complete the questions.

1. People do not come here on Sundays.

   _Do they come_____ on Saturdays?

2. Carol has class on Mondays and Wednesdays.

   _____ class on Tuesdays, too?

3. The children like bananas.

   _____ apples, too?

(continued on next page)

4. We live in a house.

_____ in a big house?

5. My boyfriend knows my brother.

_____ your sister?

6. My wife and I want a hotel room.

_____ a room for one or two nights?

7. I have two sisters.

_____ any brothers?

8. The car does not belong to Mr. Winchester.

_____ to Mrs. Winchester?

9. My classmates and I do not like grammar exercises.

_____ vocabulary exercises?

10. I do not know the answer to the first question.

_____ the answer to the second question?

11. The saleswomen do not work in the afternoon.

_____ in the morning?

12. That young man does not come from the United States.

_____ from Canada?

SIMPLE PRESENT TENSE: *WH-* QUESTIONS

 QUESTION WORDS

Write the correct question words. Use **who**, **what**, **where**, **when**, **what time**, *or* **why**.

1. __What__?   **a.** Cereal.
2. __Why__?   **b.** Because I'm tired.
3. _____?   **c.** At City Central Bank.
4. _____?   **d.** A suit and tie.
5. _____?   **e.** My teacher.
6. _____?   **f.** At noon.
7. _____?   **g.** His friends.
8. _____?   **h.** At his school.
9. _____?   **i.** In the morning.
10. _____?   **j.** Because I want to buy a sweatshirt.
11. _____?   **k.** At 6:00.
12. _____?   **l.** In August.

2 ***WH-* QUESTIONS WITH THE SIMPLE PRESENT TENSE**

Write questions. Then find an answer for each question in Exercise 1. Write the answers below.

1. want / to leave / do / why / you

   __Why do you want to leave?__   Because I'm tired.

2. for breakfast / what / you / have / do

   _____   _____

3. get up / husband / does / what time / your

   _____   _____

4. your / corrects / homework / who

   _____   _____

61

(continued on next page)

5. does / work / Rosita / where

_____   _____

6. on vacation / when / go / you and your family / do

_____   _____

7. what / to work / wear / you / do

_____   _____

8. need / do / more money / you / why

_____   _____

9. the / what time / eat / kids / do / lunch

_____   _____

10. come / the / mail / does / when

_____   _____

11. Doug / soccer / play / where / does

_____   _____

12. visit / does / on Sundays / Milt / who

_____   _____

3 QUESTION WORDS

Complete the sentences. Use **who**, **what**, **where**, **when**, **what time**,
or **why**.

ROB: Mom, I'm leaving.

MOM: _____Why?_____
        1.
ROB: I have a date.

MOM: _____ is your date?
            2.
ROB: At 8:00.

MOM: _____ do you have a date with?
            3.
ROB: With Susie.

Mom: _____ does Susie live?
      4.

Rob: On Franklin Street.

Mom: _____ does Susie do?
      5.

Rob: She's a student like me, and she has a part-time job.

Mom: _____ does she work?
      6.

Rob: On Saturdays and Sundays.

Mom: _____ does she work?
      7.

Rob: At Cerrano's—you know, the supermarket.

Mom: That's far away. _____ takes her there and picks her up?
                          8.

Rob: I don't know. Her parents, probably.

Mom: _____ do you like her?
      9.

Rob: She's nice.

Mom: Yes, but _____ do you know about her?
             10.

Rob: I know that she's nice.

4 WH- QUESTIONS WITH THE SIMPLE PRESENT TENSE

Write the questions. Use **who, what, where, when, what time,** *or* **why.**

1.   What time do you go to bed?

   I go to bed at 11:00.

2. _____

   I drive my children to school because their school is far away.

3. _____

   Pilots? They fly planes.

4. _____

   I think the bank opens at 8:30.

5. _____

   I'm studying because I have a test tomorrow.

(continued on next page)

6. _____

One of my brothers lives in New York, and the other lives in Philadelphia.

7. _____

My mother usually does the shopping, but sometimes my father does.

8. _____

I'm not sure. I think most American children start school when they're five years old.

9. _____

In the big white house? I think an old man and woman live there.

10. _____

We stay home and relax on the weekend.

11. _____

Not me. Ask Kate about your keys.

12. _____

The doctor wants to see *you* first.

SIMPLE PRESENT TENSE AND
THIS / THAT / THESE / THOSE

① *THIS* AND *THESE*

Complete the conversations. Use **this** *or* **these** *and* **is** *or* **are**.

1. **A:** _____These_____ _____are_____ my socks.

   B: No, they're not. _____These_____ _____are_____ your socks

   and _____this_____ _____is_____ your shirt.

2. **A:** _____ _____ a gift for you.

   B: Oh, thank you.

3. **A:** _____ hamburger _____ terrible.

   B: _____ potatoes _____ awful, too.

4. **A:** _____ television _____ heavy.

   B: _____ bookcase _____ heavy, too.

5. **A:** Brenda, _____ _____ Tim.

   B: Hi, Tim. It's nice to meet you.

6. **A:** _____ shoes _____ only $35.

   B: Really?

7. **A:** _____ _____ a great party.

   B: I know.

8. **A:** _____ _____ beautiful earrings.

   B: _____ bracelet _____ nice, too.

9. **A:** _____ cookies _____ for you.

   B: Gee, that's nice of you. Thanks.

10. **A:** _____ _____ my parents.

    B: Really? They're so young.

2 QUESTIONS WITH *THIS* AND *THESE*

Write questions. Use **What's this?** *or* **What are these?**

1. **A:** _What are these?_____

   B: They're trees.

2. **A:** _____

   B: It's the sun.

3. **A:** _____

   B: It's my dog.

4. **A:** _____

   B: It's a car.

5. **A:** _____

   B: They're my dolls.

6. **A:** _____

   B: They're flowers.

7. **A:** _____

   B: It's a chair.

8. **A:** _____

   B: They're balls.

9. **A:** _____

   B: They're birds.

10. **A:** _____

    B: It's a house.

3 THAT AND *THOSE*

Complete the conversation. Use **that** *or* **those**.

A: Are you enjoying the party?

B: Yes, very much. But I don't know a lot of the people. Who's _____that_____ handsome
    1.
    guy over there?

A: Do you mean the guy next to _____ bookshelf?
    2.

B: No, the guy between _____ paintings on the wall.
    3.

A: He's my cousin, Dennis.

B: And _____ two people?
    4.

A: Which people?

B: _____ people in the corner.
    5.

A: They're also my cousins.

B: Don't tell me _____ woman on the sofa is also your cousin.
    6.

A: No, _____'s my Aunt Phyllis.
    7.

B: And is _____ man next to her her husband?
    8.

A: No, _____'s her brother, my Uncle Norman.
    9.

B: What about _____ kids in the bedroom?
    10.

A: Some of them are cousins, but _____ two at the door are my sisters.
    11.

B: You have a big family. Are _____ nice-looking women near the kitchen your
    12.
    relatives, too?

A: No, the one with the blonde hair is my girlfriend, but I don't know the other woman.

4 THIS, THAT, THESE, AND THOSE

Complete the sentences. Use **this**, **that**, **these**, *or* **those**.

1. Robert and his wife are sitting in their new car. Robert says, "I like _____this_____ car."

2. Doris looks out the window and sees someone. She doesn't know the person. Doris says, "Who's _____?"

3. A friend has a gift for Ted and puts a small box in his hand. Ted says, "What's _____?"

4. Sylvia and Elizabeth are at a party. Sylvia says to Elizabeth, "Isn't _____ a great party?"

5. Vicky and Peggy are looking in the window of a shoe store. Vicky says to Penny, "Aren't _____ shoes beautiful?"

6. Vicky and Peggy are in the store now. Vicky has the shoes in her hands. Vicky says, "_____ shoes really are beautiful."

7. Mr. Graham comes into his office. He asks his secretary about some people in the waiting room. Mr. Graham says, "Are _____ people waiting for me?"

8. Richard and Sandy are looking for their car in the parking lot. Richard finally sees it. It's behind four other cars. Richard says, "_____'s our car. Do you see it?"

9. Frank is at the kitchen table. There's a dish of potatoes in front of him. Frank says to his brother, "_____ are my potatoes. Don't eat them."

10. Mr. and Mrs. Moreno are in their car. They're lost. Mr. Moreno sees a sign about fifty meters away. He asks his wife, "What does _____ sign say?"

SIMPLE PRESENT TENSE AND ONE / ONES AND IT

ONE AND ONES

Match the sentences and responses.

1. __d__ Do you want the big box?   **a.** No, it's dirty. Take this one.

2. ____ I like the black pants.   **b.** Which one?

3. ____ Is this towel for me?   **c.** The brown ones.

4. ____ I like the sneakers.   **d.** No, give me the small one.

5. ____ Please give me that eraser.   **e.** No, I want the chocolate chip ones.

6. ____ Which shoes do you like?   **f.** Yes, there's one on Broadway.

7. ____ Are there any movie theaters near here?   **g.** I don't. I like the gray ones.

     h. Which ones?

8. ____ Do you want the raisin cookies?

② ONE, ONES, AND *IT*

Add **one**, **ones**, *or* **it** *where necessary.*

1. **A:** Which is your car?

   B: The blue ⌃one.

2. **A:** Do you want the black shoes?

   B: No, I prefer the brown.

3. **A:** Please bring that chair over here.

   B: The in the corner?

   A: Yes, please.

4. **A:** Do you need all the eggs?

   B: No, only the in the bowl.

5. **A:** This apple is good.

   B: You're lucky. This is terrible.

6. **A:** Is there a supermarket near here?

   B: No, but there's about a mile away.

7. **A:** Which pills do you want?

   B: The on the kitchen table.

8. **A:** Do you want a hamburger?

   B: No, but Carla wants.

9. **A:** I like the new Rockets CD.

   B: Yeah. I like, too.

10. **A:** These cherries are good.

    B: The other are better.

11. **A:** Do you want these sandwiches?

    B: No, give me the over there.

12. **A:** I like this apartment.

    B: But the on Fifth Street costs less.

13. **A:** I want to buy some earrings.

    B: Do you want the gold earrings or the silver?

14. **A:** Where's my cell phone?

    B: Is on the table near the door.

SIMPLE PAST TENSE: REGULAR VERBS—AFFIRMATIVE AND NEGATIVE STATEMENTS

1 AFFIRMATIVE AND NEGATIVE STATEMENTS WITH THE SIMPLE PAST TENSE

Match the sentences.

1. __d__ Sylvia is tired.

2. ____ Sylvia's worried about her French test.

3. ____ Sylvia's car is clean.

4. ____ Sylvia is hungry.

5. ____ Sylvia is angry.

6. ____ Sylvia is happy.

7. ____ Sylvia's talking about a TV program.

8. ____ Sylvia's grandparents are unhappy.

9. ____ There's a lot of food in Sylvia's refrigerator.

a. She washed it yesterday.

b. Her boyfriend called her yesterday to say, "I love you."

c. She watched it last night.

d. She didn't sleep much last night.

e. She didn't eat breakfast or lunch.

f. She didn't visit them last weekend.

g. Her boyfriend forgot her birthday.

h. She cooked a lot yesterday.

i. She didn't study very much.

② PAST TIME MARKERS

Complete the sentences. Use **yesterday** *or* **last**.

Detective's Notes on Mr. Horace Smith

April 15th   Traveled to Vancouver

April 25th   Borrowed $20,000

May 13th   Moved into a new apartment

(Nothing unusual until May 19th)

May 19th

     7:00 A.M.   Arrived at work

     2:00 P.M.   Finished work

     6:00 P.M.   Returned to the office

     11:00 P.M.   Visited someone at a hotel

It's Thursday, May 20th. Here's our report on Horace Smith.

___Last___ month he traveled to Vancouver. _____ month he also
  1.   **2.**

borrowed $20,000 from the bank. _____ week he moved into a new apartment.
                                         3.

_____ morning he arrived at work at seven o'clock. At two o'clock
  4.

_____ afternoon he finished work. Then something strange happened. He
  5.

returned to the office at six o'clock _____ evening and visited someone at a hotel
                                        6.

at eleven o'clock _____ night.
               7.

3 SIMPLE PAST TENSE AND *AGO*

Answer the questions.

a. What day of the week is it today? _____

b. What month is it now? _____

c. What year is it now? _____

Use the answers above to rewrite the sentences. Use **ago**.

1. Eric cleaned his apartment last Sunday. (*It is Tuesday.*)

   _____Eric cleaned his apartment two days ago._____

2. Eric traveled to Poland in 1999.

   _____

3. Eric visited his college roommate last July.

   _____

4. Eric called his parents last Monday.

   _____

5. Eric talked to his boss about a raise last Friday.

   _____

6. Eric graduated from college in 1996.

   _____

7. Eric moved to Georgia last December.

   _____

8. Eric played tennis last Thursday.

   _____

9. Eric studied Polish in 1997.

   _____

10. Eric's grandfather died last September.

   _____

④ AFFIRMATIVE STATEMENTS WITH THE SIMPLE PAST TENSE

Complete the sentences. Use subject pronouns.

1. Pete walks to work every day.

   _____He walked to work_____ yesterday, too.

2. Lenny, Mike, and Warren play basketball every Saturday.

   _____ last Saturday, too.

3. Ellen washes her clothes every Sunday.

   _____ last Sunday, too.

4. My classmates study every night.

   _____ last night, too.

5. Robert works in his garden every weekend.

   _____ last weekend, too.

6. Norma prepares dinner at 6:00 every day.

   _____ yesterday, too.

7. Anna talks to her daughter every Friday night.

   _____ last Friday night, too.

8. Michele and her husband travel to France every summer.

   _____ last summer, too.

9. The bank closes at 3:00 P.M. every day.

   _____ yesterday, too.

10. Adam and his sister watch television every night.

    _____ last night, too.

5 AFFIRMATIVE AND NEGATIVE STATEMENTS WITH THE SIMPLE PAST TENSE

Complete the sentences. Use the correct form of the verbs in parentheses.

1. I _____washed_____ the clothes this morning, but I
   (wash)
   _____didn't wash_____ the dishes.
   (not wash)

2. We _____ the Hangs to our party last week, but we
   (invite)
   _____ the Lees.
   (not invite)

3. I _____ the kitchen yesterday, but I
   (clean)
   _____ the bathroom.
   (not clean)

4. Last night I _____ to my aunt, but I
   (talk)
   _____ to my uncle.
   (not talk)

5. I _____ your brother a few minutes ago, but I
   (call)
   _____ you.
   (not call)

6. We _____ television last night, but we
   (watch)
   _____ the news.
   (not watch)

7. Mr. Lugo _____ his book to the library today, but
   (return)
   Mrs. Lugo _____ hers.
   (not return)

8. The artist _____ a picture of her sister, but she
   (paint)
   _____ a picture of her brother.
   (not paint)

9. I _____ some potatoes, but I
   (cook)
   _____ any meat.
   (not cook)

10. I _____ history in high school, but I
    (study)
    _____ geography.
    (not study)

6 VERB TENSE REVIEW: PRESENT PROGRESSIVE, SIMPLE PRESENT, AND SIMPLE PAST

Complete the letter. Use the simple present, present progressive, or simple past tense of the verbs in parentheses.

April 12

Dear Amira,

I _____am sitting_____ at my desk, and I _____ of you. I often
   1. (sit)   **2. (think)**

_____ of you on days like today. The sun _____, and
   3. (think)   **4. (shine)**

the birds _____.
              5. (sing)

   The weather's very different from the weather yesterday. It _____ all
                                                                  6. (rain)

day long and I _____ in the house from morning until night.
                  7. (stay)

I _____ out at all. I _____ the clothes and
   8. (not go)   **9. (wash)**

_____ the house—very exciting! After dinner, I _____
   10. (clean)   **11. (play)**

cards with some neighbors.

   One of my neighbors, Alfredo, _____ from Argentina. Sometimes
                                     12. (come)

I _____ Spanish with him. I _____ Spanish very
   13. (speak)   **14. (not speak)**

well, but Alfredo is very nice and never _____ at my mistakes.
                                             15. (laugh)

   Last week he _____ me to an Argentinian party. We
                    16. (invite)

_____ to beautiful music all night and I _____ a lot.
   17. (listen)   **18. (dance)**

I really _____ myself.
            19. (enjoy)

   Well, it's time to go. I _____ some Argentinian food, and
                              20. (cook)

I _____ to check it. I _____ it to burn. You and I
   21. (need)   **22. (not want)**

both _____ that I'm not a very good cook!
        23. (know)

   Write soon!

Love,

Connie

SIMPLE PAST TENSE: IRREGULAR VERBS—AFFIRMATIVE AND NEGATIVE STATEMENTS

1 REGULAR AND IRREGULAR VERBS

Underline the simple past tense verb in each sentence. Write **regular** *if it is regular. Write* **irregular** *if it is irregular. Then write the base form of the verb.*

1. This morning I <u>got</u> up at seven o'clock.   irregular   get

2. I <u>washed</u> my face and hands.   regular   wash

3. Then I put on my clothes.   _____   _____

4. I had orange juice and toast for breakfast.   _____   _____

5. After breakfast I brushed my teeth.   _____   _____

6. I left the house at 7:45.   _____   _____

7. I arrived at school at 8:15.   _____   _____

8. Class began at 8:30.   _____   _____

9. We learned some new grammar rules in class today.   _____   _____

10. Class finished at 11:30.   _____   _____

11. I met some friends for lunch.   _____   _____

12. We ate at a pizza place.   _____   _____

13. After lunch we went to a swimming pool.   _____   _____

14. We stayed there until four o'clock.   _____   _____

❷ AFFIRMATIVE STATEMENTS WITH THE SIMPLE PAST TENSE OF IRREGULAR VERBS

Complete each sentence with the simple past tense form of the verb.

1. I didn't eat eggs for breakfast. I _____*ate*_____ cereal.

2. We didn't drink coffee. We _____ tea.

3. He didn't leave at six o'clock. He _____ at seven.

4. She didn't meet her sister at the movies. She _____ her brother at the park.

5. I didn't speak to the waiter. I _____ to the manager.

6. I didn't go to the supermarket on Walnut Street. I _____ to the supermarket on Chestnut Street.

7. The thief didn't steal my money. He _____ my jewelry.

8. I didn't find your keys. I _____ your address book.

9. We didn't drive to the park. We _____ to the beach.

10. I didn't see Carol. I _____ Yoko.

11. My husband didn't bring me flowers. He _____ me chocolates.

12. We didn't come by bus. We _____ by taxi.

13. I didn't read a newspaper. I _____ a magazine.

14. I didn't send a letter to my cousin. I _____ a postcard to my friend.

15. He didn't forget his notebook in the car. He _____ it at school.

3 NEGATIVE STATEMENTS WITH THE SIMPLE PAST TENSE OF IRREGULAR VERBS

Write true sentences.

1. I / become / an English teacher / last year

    I didn't become an English teacher last year.

2. I / eat / three kilos of oranges for breakfast / yesterday morning

_____

3. I / sleep / twenty-one hours / yesterday

_____

4. I / bring / a horse to English class / two weeks ago

_____

5. I / go / to the moon / last month

_____

6. I / meet / the leader of my country / last night

_____

7. I / find / $10,000 in a brown paper bag / yesterday

_____

8. I / do / this exercise / two years ago

_____

9. I / swim / thirty kilometers / yesterday

_____

10. I / speak / English perfectly / ten years ago

_____

④ AFFIRMATIVE AND NEGATIVE STATEMENTS WITH THE SIMPLE PAST TENSE

Complete the diary. Use the simple past tense form of the verbs in parentheses.

> I ___had___ a nice day today. I _____ up until ten o'clock,
> 1. (have)   2. (not get)
>
> so I _____ dressed quickly and _____ to the Fine Arts
>   3. (get)   4. (go)
>
> Museum.
>
> I _____ Cindy and Frank there, and we _____ into
>   5. (meet)   6. (go)
>
> the museum to see a new exhibit. We _____ everything because
>   7. (not see)
>
> we _____ enough time. The exhibit _____ at one o'clock.
>   8. (not have)   9. (close)
>
> We _____ at a Chinese restaurant near the museum, and then
>   10. (eat)
>
> we _____ a bus to the Downtown Shopping Mall. We
>   11. (take)
>
> _____ at the mall for a couple of hours and _____
>   12. (stay)   13. (look)
>
> around. I _____ a new shirt, but Frank and Cindy
>   14. (buy)
>
> _____ anything.
>   15. (not buy)
>
> Cindy and Frank _____ back home with me, and I
>   16. (come)
>
> _____ dinner here. I _____ much in the refrigerator, so I
>   17. (make)   18. (not have)
>
> _____ to the supermarket to get some things. I _____
>   19. (drive)   20. (see)
>
> Ramón there and _____ him for dinner, too.
>   21. (invite)
>
> We _____ until late, and after dinner we _____ a
>   22. (not eat)   23. (watch)
>
> video. Ramón, Cindy, and Frank _____ until after midnight.
>   24. (not leave)
>
> It's one o'clock in the morning now, and I'm tired. It's time to go to bed.
>
> Good night!

SIMPLE PAST TENSE: YES / NO AND WH- QUESTIONS

 YES / NO QUESTIONS AND SHORT ANSWERS WITH THE SIMPLE PAST TENSE

Answer the questions. Use short answers. (Look at the conversation on pages 148–149 of your Student Book if you need help.)

1. Did Carol have Thanksgiving dinner with her family?

No, she didn't.

2. Did Carol and Yoko go to San Francisco for Thanksgiving?

_____

3. Did Elenore make a turkey for Thanksgiving?

_____

4. Did Pete prepare anything for the Thanksgiving dinner?

_____

5. Did Norma have Thanksgiving dinner with her family?

_____

6. Did Pete and Uncle Bob have a fight on Thanksgiving?

_____

7. Did Uncle Bob like Pete's soup?

_____

8. Did Pete and Elenore have Thanksgiving dinner at their home?

_____

9. Did Uncle Bob watch a football game on television?

_____

2 *YES / NO* **QUESTIONS AND SHORT ANSWERS WITH THE SIMPLE PAST TENSE**

There's a mistake in each question. Write the questions without the mistakes. Then answer them. Use short answers.

1. You did finish the last exercise?

    Did you finish the last exercise?

    Yes, I did. (OR: No, I didn't.)

2. Did you all the homework?

    _____

    _____

3. You did took a bath this morning?

    _____

    _____

4. Does your best friend come over to your house last night?

    _____

    _____

5. Did you went to bed early last night?

    _____

    _____

6. Did your English teacher taught you new grammar last week?

    _____

    _____

7. Do you visit the United States ten years ago?

    _____

    _____

8. Did your mother and father got married a long time ago?

    _____

    _____

9. Did you watched television last night?

    _____

    _____

3 **AFFIRMATIVE STATEMENTS AND** *YES / NO* **QUESTIONS WITH THE SIMPLE PAST TENSE**

Look at Sharon's list. Write her husband's questions. Then complete each answer. Use the simple past tense form of the verbs in parentheses.

THINGS TO DO

Get the clothes from the dry cleaners

Buy food for dinner

Meet Glen for lunch

Write a letter to Rena

Go to the bank

Return the book to the library

Look for a birthday present for Jane

Call the doctor

Bake some cookies

Pick the children up at 4:00

SHARON: Steven, you always say I forget to do things. Well, today I remembered to do

everything.

STEVEN: Are you sure? Let's see your list.   Did you get the clothes from the dry cleaners?
                                                                                            1.

SHARON: Uh-huh. I _____put_____ them in the closet.
                              2. (put)

STEVEN: _____
                                                          3.

SHARON: Yes, I did. I _____ some chicken, some vegetables,
                                              4. (get)

and some apples for dessert.

(continued on next page)

STEVEN: _____
5.

SHARON: Yeah. We _____ at a great Thai restaurant.
6. (eat)

STEVEN: _____
7.

SHARON: Yes. I _____ it at the post office.
8. (mail)

STEVEN: _____
9.

SHARON: Yes, I did. I _____ both of the checks.
10. (deposit)

STEVEN: _____
11.

SHARON: Yes, I did. And I _____ out another book by the
12. (take)

same author.

STEVEN: _____
13.

SHARON: Yeah. I _____ her a sweater.
14. (buy)

STEVEN: _____
15.

SHARON: Uh-huh. He _____ all the test results are fine.
16. (say)

STEVEN: _____
17.

SHARON: Of course. And I _____ a few already. They're
18. (have)

delicious.

STEVEN: _____
19.

SHARON: Oh no, I _____! What time is it?
20. (forget)

4 WH- QUESTIONS WITH THE SIMPLE PAST TENSE

Match the questions and answers about Carol and Yoko's Thanksgiving holiday.

1. __f__ Who drove from Oregon to San Francisco?

2. _____ Where did Yoko and Carol rent the car?

3. _____ When did Yoko and Carol arrive in San Francisco?

4. _____ How long did it take to drive from Oregon to San Francisco?

5. _____ What did they do on Thursday?

6. _____ Where did they walk on Friday?

7. _____ Who invited Yoko and Carol to his home?

8. _____ Who did they walk around Berkeley with?

9. _____ Why didn't Carol and Yoko visit Yoko's uncle?

a. More than six hours.

b. Around Berkeley.

c. On Wednesday night.

d. Because they didn't want to drive anymore.

e. Yoko's uncle.

f. Yoko and Carol did.

g. They visited Fisherman's Wharf.

h. Yoko's friends.

i. In Oregon.

5 WH- QUESTIONS WITH THE SIMPLE PAST TENSE

Write questions. Then answer them. (If you need help, the answers are at the end of the exercise, but they are not in order.)

1. Where / Americans / celebrate Thanksgiving / for the first time

   Where did Americans celebrate Thanksgiving for the first time?

   In Massachusetts.

2. When / a person / walk on the moon / for the first time

   _____

   _____

3. What / William Shakespeare / write

   _____

   _____

(continued on next page)

4. Where / the Olympic games / start

_____

_____

5. Why / many people / go to California / in 1849

_____

_____

6. How long / John F. Kennedy / live in the White House

_____

_____

7. What / Alfred Hitchcock / make

_____

_____

8. Why / the Chinese / build the Great Wall

_____

_____

9. How long / World War II / last in Europe

_____

_____

10. When / Christopher Columbus / discover / America

_____

_____

Almost three years.
About six years.
In 1969.
In 1492.
In Greece.
In Massachusetts.
Movies.
Plays like *Romeo and Juliet.*
They wanted to keep foreigners out of the country.
They wanted to find gold.

6 QUESTIONS WITH *WHO* AS SUBJECT OR OBJECT

Write questions. Use **who** *and the verb in parentheses.*

1. **A:** Carol went to San Francisco.

   B: _____Who did she go_____ with?
   <u>(go)</u>
   A: With her roommate, Yoko.

   B: How did they go there?

   A: By car.

   B: _____Who drove_____?
   <u>(drive)</u>
   A: I don't know. Probably both of them.

2. **A:** Those are beautiful flowers. _____ them to you?
   <u>(give)</u>
   B: My boyfriend.

3. **A:** I went to a party at my old high school last night.

   B: _____ there?
   <u>(see)</u>
4. **A:** You got a phone call a couple of minutes ago.

   B: _____?
   <u>(call)</u>
   A: A woman. Her name was Betty Kowalski.

5. **A:** Did you ever read the book *The Old Man and the Sea*?

   B: _____ it?
   <u>(write)</u>
   A: Ernest Hemingway.

6. **A:** Where are the children?

   B: At Ryan Santiago's house.

   A: _____ them there?
   <u>(take)</u>
   B: Ryan's mother.

7. **A:** My wife sent the money to your office a month ago.

   B: _____ it to?
   <u>(send)</u>
   A: Nicole Sanda.

(continued on next page)

8. A: The car is so clean. _____ it?
(clean)

   B: I took it to a car wash.

   A: It looks great.

9. A: Did you hear the news? Kay got married.

   B: Really? _____?
(marry)

   A: A guy from Oklahoma. I don't know his name.

10. A: My grandparents went to Arizona for two months last winter.

   B: _____ with?
(stay)

   A: My cousin, Howard. He has a big house there.

❼ WH- QUESTIONS WITH THE SIMPLE PAST TENSE

Complete the conversation between a detective and a suspect. Write questions. Use **what**, **where**, **when**, **who**, *or* **why**.

DETECTIVE: There was a robbery last night, and someone said you did it.

SUSPECT: That person's lying.

DETECTIVE: Well, then. Tell us about your activities last night.

   What did you do? _____
1.

SUSPECT: We went to the movies.

DETECTIVE: We? _____
2.

SUSPECT: A friend. Her name's Wendy Kaufman.

DETECTIVE: _____
3.

SUSPECT: I left home at around 5:30.

DETECTIVE: _____
4.

SUSPECT: The movie started at 8:30.

DETECTIVE: _____
5.

SUSPECT: I left my house so early because we had dinner before the movie.

DETECTIVE: _____
6.

SUSPECT: At Maxi's Steak House.

DETECTIVE: _____
7.

SUSPECT: I met her at the restaurant.

DETECTIVE: _____
8.

SUSPECT: A steak. That's what everybody eats at Maxi's.

DETECTIVE: We're not interested in everybody. We're only interested in you.

_____
9.

SUSPECT: The waitress saw us, of course. And I talked to the manager, too.

DETECTIVE: _____
10.

SUSPECT: Because the steak was no good.

DETECTIVE: _____
11.

SUSPECT: After dinner? To the movies. I told you that already.

DETECTIVE: _____
12.

SUSPECT: *Wine and Roses.* You know, the movie with Kristie McNeil.

DETECTIVE: _____
13.

SUSPECT: At the Cinemax on Ocean Road.

21 IMPERATIVES; SUGGESTIONS WITH LET'S, WHY DON'T WE . . . ?; WHY DON'T YOU . . . ?

1 AFFIRMATIVE AND NEGATIVE IMPERATIVES

Match the people with their statements.

1. __d__ The teacher said,
2. ____ Mr. Michaels told his children,
3. ____ The doctor said,
4. ____ The police officer said,
5. ____ Jenny told her brother,

a. "Leave me alone."
b. "Open your mouth and say, 'Ah.' "
c. "Put your hands up."
d. "Open your books to page 34."
e. "Go to bed."

Then do the same with these statements.

6. ____ The teacher said,
7. ____ Mr. Michaels told his children,
8. ____ The doctor said,
9. ____ The police officer said,
10. ____ Jenny told her brother,

f. "Don't move."
g. "Don't eat so fast."
h. "Don't bother me."
i. "Don't talk during the test."
j. "Don't take this medicine at night."

2 AFFIRMATIVE AND NEGATIVE IMPERATIVES

Complete the sentences. Use the verbs in the box. Add **Don't** *where necessary.*

ask	be	buy	clean	give
~~go~~	~~open~~	study	talk	tell
use	touch			

1. I'm hot. Please _____open_____ the window.

2. That animal is dangerous. _____Don't go_____ near it.

3. _____ your room right now. It's a mess.

4. The baby is asleep. _____ so loudly.

5. The apples look bad. _____ them.

6. We're lost. _____ the police officer for directions.

7. It's a surprise party. _____ late.

8. This is a secret. _____ anyone.

9. The test is on Monday. _____ pages 50 and 51.

10. I'm cold. _____ me my sweater, please.

11. This glass isn't yours. _____ it.

12. The stove is hot. _____ it.

3 AFFIRMATIVE IMPERATIVES

Look at the map and complete the note. Use the verbs in the box.

get off   go   make   ring   ~~take~~   turn   walk

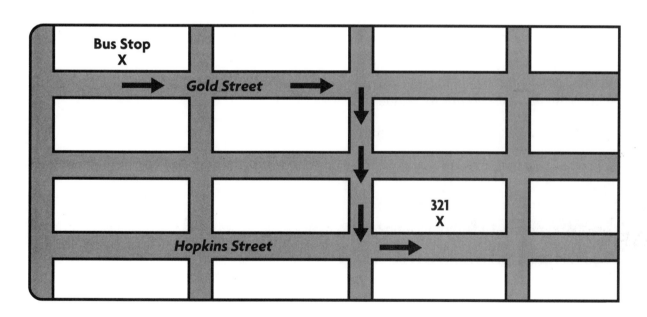

DIRECTIONS

_____Take_____ bus twenty-six. _____ the
　　　1.　　　　　　　　　　　　　　　　　2.
bus on Gold Street. _____ down Gold Street. At the traffic light,
　　　　　　　　3.
_____ a right. _____ another two
　　4.　　　　　　　　　　　　　　5.
blocks. Then _____ a left turn. That's Hopkins Street.
　　　　　　　6.
_____ the bell at 321 Hopkins. That's my house.
　7.

4 LET'S AND *WHY DON'T WE . . . ?*

Complete the sentences. Circle the correct answers and write them on the lines.

1. Students in an English class say to the teacher, "_____ Let's take a break. _____"

   a. Let's take a break.

   b. Let's take a test.

2. Donny says to his brother, "_____"

   a. Why don't we clean our room?

   b. Why don't we play basketball?

3. It's Saturday night, and Pete and Elenore are tired. Elenore says,

   "_____"

   a. Let's go dancing tonight.

   b. Let's not do anything tonight.

4. It's five o'clock. One secretary says to another secretary,

   "_____"

   a. Why don't we go out for dinner?

   b. Why don't we work late tonight?

5. Two tourists are in a foreign country. One tourist says to the other,

   "_____"

   a. Why don't we visit a museum?

   b. Why don't we sleep all day?

6. Louisa thinks TV is boring. She says to her boyfriend,

   "_____"

   a. Let's not watch TV tonight.

   b. Let's watch TV tonight.

7. It's a beautiful day. Miriam says to her roommate, "_____"

   a. Let's not forget our umbrellas.

   b. Let's not take the car to class today. Let's walk.

8. It's Pete Winston's birthday. Carol says to Norma, "_____"

   a. Why don't we get a present for Dad?

   b. Why don't we forget about Dad's birthday?

9. Celia and her sister are late. Celia says, "_____"

   a. Let's take a taxi.

   b. Let's walk.

10. It's cold. Jenny says to her boyfriend, "_____"

   a. Let's wait outside.

   b. Let's not wait outside.

⑤ LET'S AND *WHY DON'T WE . . . ?*

Write sentences. Use **let's** *and the expressions in the box.*

get something to eat	go swimming	leave
go inside	~~go to bed~~	not invite her to the party
go out and look for him		

1. A: I'm tired.

   B: I am, too.

   A: Let's go to bed.   _____

2. A: I'm hungry.

   B: I am, too.

   A: _____

3. A: I'm hot.

   B: I am, too.

   A: _____

4. A: I'm angry with Lulu.

   B: I am, too.

   A: _____

(continued on next page)

*Write sentences. Use **Why don't we . . . ?** and the expressions in the box.*

5. A: I'm worried about Rocky. Where is he?

   B: I don't know.

   A: _____

6. A: I'm cold.

   B: I am, too.

   A: _____

7. A: I'm bored at this party.

   B: I am, too.

   A: _____

6 WHY DON'T YOU . . . ?

Match the sentences and responses.

__c__ **1.** I'm tired.

_____ **2.** I don't know the meaning of this word.

_____ **3.** I don't know what to do tonight.

_____ **4.** I'm hungry.

_____ **5.** I'm hot.

a. Why don't you make a sandwich?

b. Why don't you go to the movies?

c. Why don't you go to bed?

d. Why don't you open the window?

e. Why don't you look it up in your dictionary?

*Write your own responses with **Why don't you . . . ?***

6. I'm bored. _____

7. I want to practice English more. _____

8. I have a headache. _____

SUBJECT AND OBJECT PRONOUNS; DIRECT AND INDIRECT OBJECTS

❶ OBJECTS

Underline the object in each sentence.

1. Please help <u>Yoko and Carol</u>.

2. Peter loves his daughter.

3. Read page 104.

4. Don't ask the teacher.

5. Don't eat my ice cream.

6. Buy five stamps.

❷ OBJECT PRONOUNS

Underline the object pronoun in each sentence.

1. Don't tell <u>him</u>.

2. We love you very much.

3. My mother loves me very much.

4. Put it in our car.

5. Meet her later.

6. My mom sent it.

7. Why don't you help them?

8. They e-mailed us.

3 SUBJECT PRONOUNS, POSSESSIVE ADJECTIVES, AND OBJECT PRONOUNS

Complete the chart.

	SUBJECT PRONOUNS	POSSESSIVE ADJECTIVES	OBJECT PRONOUNS
	(*I* am here.)	(This is *my* book.)	(Help *me*.)
1.	I	my	
2.		your	you
3.	he		him
4.		her	
5.	it		
6.		our	
7.	they		

4 OBJECT PRONOUNS

Complete the sentences. Use **me**, **you**, **him**, **her**, **our**, *or* **them**.

1. **A:** Is this for Lulu and Bertha?

   B: Yes, it's for _____them_____.

2. **A:** Is this for me?

   B: Yes, it's for _____.

3. **A:** Is this for Milt?

   B: Yes, it's for _____.

4. **A:** Is this for my sister?

   B: Yes, it's for _____.

5. **A:** Is this for you?

   B: Yes, it's for _____.

6. **A:** Is this for her father?

   B: Yes, it's for _____.

7. **A:** Is this for you and me?

   B: Yes, it's for _____.

8. **A:** Is this for the dogs?

   B: Yes, it's for _____.

9. **A:** Is this for the children?

   B: Yes, it's for _____.

10. **A:** Is this for your grandmother?

    B: Yes, it's for _____.

11. **A:** Is this for Yoko?

    B: Yes, it's for _____.

12. **A:** Is this for my classmates and me?

    B: Yes, it's for _____.

5 SUBJECT AND OBJECT PRONOUNS

Unscramble the word groups to write sentences. Use correct punctuation and capitalization.

1. love / you / I ___I love you.___

2. him / she / loves _____

3. us / love / they _____

4. we / them / love _____

5. the answer / tell / me _____

6. show / her / the paper _____

7. them / take / some flowers _____

8. me / a postcard / send _____

6 SUBJECT AND OBJECT PRONOUNS

Complete the sentences. Use a subject pronoun or an object pronoun.

1. A: Is your name Doug?

    B: Yes, _____it_____ is.

2. A: This record is for you. _____'s for your birthday.

    B: Oh, thank you. I love _____.

3. A: Is Bertha your aunt?

    B: Yes, _____ is.

    A: Please give _____ this package.

4. A: My brother is over there.

    B: I like _____. _____ is handsome.

5. A: Are you busy?

    B: Yes, _____ am. Please call _____ later.

6. A: Here are two dishes.

    B: But _____'re dirty. Please wash _____.

(continued on next page)

7. **A:** Are you and Lee free on Sunday?

   B: Yes, _____ are. Visit _____ then.

8. **A:** Hello?

   B: Hello. Is Judi there?

   A: Yes. Just a minute. Judi! Judi! The phone's for _____.

7 DIRECT AND INDIRECT OBJECT WORD ORDER

Who probably said each of the sentences? Match the sentences and speakers.

1. __f__ "Please show me your driver's license."
2. _____ "I explained the answers to you in the last class."
3. _____ "Please send this letter to Korea."
4. _____ "Let's e-mail this joke to Bill. It's funny."
5. _____ "Please pass me the salt and pepper."
6. _____ "Read the story again to me, please."
7. _____ "Give me your passport, please."
8. _____ "I sent the information to you two days ago."

   a. an immigration officer
   b. a child
   c. a restaurant customer
   d. someone at an office
   e. a teacher
   f. a police officer
   g. a post office customer
   h. a friend

8 DIRECT AND INDIRECT OBJECT WORD ORDER

Write the direct object and indirect object in each sentence in Exercise 7.

	Direct Object	Indirect Object
1.	your driver's license	me
2.		
3.		
4.		
5.		
6.		
7.		
8.		

9 INDIRECT AND DIRECT OBJECT WORD ORDER

It was Christmas a few days ago. Bernie gave the following presents to his family and friends.

Lucy ....a sweater	
Bob ....a CD	
his brother ....a video game	
Marge ....some earrings	
His grandfather ....some pajamas	
Bill ....a book	
his cousin ....some sunglasses	
his girlfriend ....a ring	

Write sentences about Bernie. Use the information in the box. Put the indirect object before the direct object.

1.   Bernie gave Lucy a sweater. _____

2.   He gave _____

3.   _____

4.   _____

Write more sentences about Bernie. Use the information in the box. Put the direct object before the indirect object.

5.   He gave some pajamas to his grandfather. _____

6.   _____

7.   _____

8.   _____

10 DIRECT AND INDIRECT OBJECT PRONOUNS

Complete the sentences. Use the correct preposition and **it**, **them**, **me**, **him**, *or* **her**.

1. This is Carol's book. Give ___it to her._____

2. This is Pete and Elenore's invitation. Send _____

3. These are Bertha's bananas. Give _____

(continued on next page)

4. Those are my keys. Hand _____

5. I need the salt. Pass _____

6. Bertha and Lulu want to see the newspaper. Show _____

⑪ DIRECT AND INDIRECT OBJECT WORD ORDER

Unscramble the word groups to write sentences. Use correct punctuation and capitalization.

1. lent / him / some money / I

    I lent him some money.

2. to / some money / I / him / lent

_____

3. the women / the man / something / is / to / showing

_____

4. them / she / some help / gives / always

_____

5. you / tell / the answer / him / did / ?

_____

6. all my friends / birthday cards / I / send

_____

7. to / the ball / me / throw

_____

8. this sentence / us / didn't / you / to / explain

_____

9. me / he / fifty dollars / owes

THERE IS / THERE ARE / IS THERE . . . ? / ARE THERE . . . ?

AFFIRMATIVE STATEMENTS WITH *THERE IS* AND *THERE ARE*

Complete the conversation. Use **there is** *or* **there are**.

A: Is anyone in the house?

B: Yes, __*there are*__ two men. _____ also a woman. Oh,
        1.   **2.**
_____ two little boys, too.
   3.

A: And in the yard?

B: _____ a dog, and _____ three other children.
   4.   **5.**

A: What's in the garage?

B: _____ some boxes.
   6.

A: What's in them?

B: I don't know, but _____ also a motorcycle. _____
                 7.   **8.**
two cars, too.

A: Two?

B: Uh-huh. _____ a TV there, too.
        9.

A: A TV? In the garage? That's strange.

B: And _____ a sofa.
    10.

A: That's really strange!

2 AFFIRMATIVE STATEMENTS WITH *THERE IS* AND *THERE ARE*

Unscramble the word groups to write sentences. Use correct punctuation and capitalization.

1. clothes / the closet / are / in / there

    There are clothes in the closet.

2. is / the table / a / there / on / knife

_____

3. the garage / there / cars / in / are / two

_____

4. flowers / there / the garden / in / are

_____

5. dog / the bed / is / under / a / there

_____

6. between / there / the two chairs / a / is / box

_____

7. is / there / the wall / a / on / picture

_____

8. are / five / there / the floor / books / on

_____

9. seven / in / there / this / house / rooms / are

_____

③ AFFIRMATIVE STATEMENTS WITH *THERE IS AND THERE ARE*

What's unusual about the tree? Write sentences. Use **there is** *or* **there are**.

1. _There is a telephone in the tree._

2. _There are suitcases in the tree._

3. _____

4. _____

5. _____

6. _____

7. _____

8. _____

9. _____

10. _____

11. _____

12. _____

13. _____

4 **AFFIRMATIVE AND NEGATIVE STATEMENTS WITH *THERE IS, THERE ISN'T, THERE ARE,* AND *THERE AREN'T***

Write sentences about Vacation Hotel. Use **there is**, **there isn't**, **there are**, *or* **there aren't**.

VACATION HOTEL

In every room:
- a bathroom
- two beds
- two closets
- a television
- an air conditioner

At the hotel:
- two restaurants
- four tennis courts
- two parking lots

1. (a bathroom in every room) ___There is a bathroom in every room.___

2. (a radio in every room) ___There isn't a radio in every room.___

3. (two beds in every room) _____

4. (two closets in every room) _____

5. (a telephone in every room) _____

6. (a television in every room) _____

7. (an air conditioner in every room) _____

8. (a refrigerator in every room) _____

9. (a swimming pool at the hotel) _____

10. (two restaurants at the hotel) _____

11. (four tennis courts at the hotel) _____

12. (gift shops at the hotel) _____

13. (two parking lots at the hotel) _____

5 **AFFIRMATIVE AND NEGATIVE STATEMENTS WITH *THERE ARE*, *THERE AREN'T*, *THEY ARE*, AND *THEY AREN'T***

Write sentences. Use **there are**, **there aren't**, **they are**, *or* **they aren't** *and the information below.*

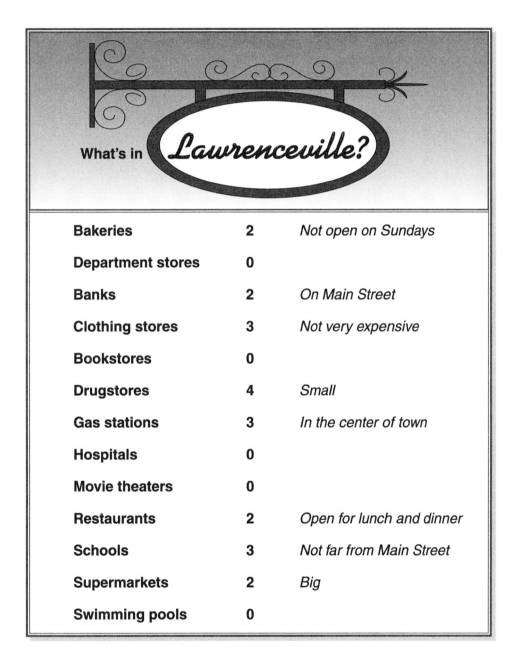

What's in Lawrenceville?		
Bakeries	2	Not open on Sundays
Department stores	0	
Banks	2	On Main Street
Clothing stores	3	Not very expensive
Bookstores	0	
Drugstores	4	Small
Gas stations	3	In the center of town
Hospitals	0	
Movie theaters	0	
Restaurants	2	Open for lunch and dinner
Schools	3	Not far from Main Street
Supermarkets	2	Big
Swimming pools	0	

1. There are two bakeries. They aren't open on Sundays.

2. There aren't any department stores.

3. _____

4. _____

5. _____

(continued on next page)

6. _____

7. _____

8. _____

9. _____

10. _____

11. _____

12. _____

13. _____

6 YES / NO QUESTIONS WITH *ARE THERE* AND SHORT ANSWERS

Look at the picture. Answer the questions. Use short answers.

1. Are there any apples? ___Yes, there are._____

2. Are there any pears? _____

3. Are there any grapes? _____

4. Are there any cherries? _____

5. Are there any strawberries? _____

6. Are there any lemons? _____

7. Are there any pineapples? _____

8. Are there any watermelons? _____

9. Are there any grapefruits? _____

---

7 **YES / NO QUESTIONS WITH *IS THERE* AND *ARE THERE* AND SHORT ANSWERS**

Write questions. Then answer them.

1. many elephants in Florida

_____Are there many elephants in Florida?_____   _____No, there aren't._____

2. many elephants in India

_____   _____

3. a desert in Canada

_____   _____

4. camels in Saudi Arabia

_____   _____

5. a long river in the Sahara Desert

_____   _____

6. many lions in Russia

_____   _____

7. mountains in Kenya

_____   _____

8. many people in Antarctica

_____   _____

9. big city in Thailand

_____   _____

10. a monkey in your garden

_____   _____

NUMBERS, QUANTIFIERS, AND QUESTIONS WITH *HOW MANY . . . ?*

① NUMBERS AND QUANTIFIERS

Put a check (✓) next to the correct sentence for each number.

1. Thirty eggs
   a. There are a few eggs in the refrigerator. _____
   b. There are a lot of eggs in the refrigerator. ✓

2. Three books
   a. There are several books on the desk. _____
   b. There are many books on the desk. _____

3. Zero people
   a. There are not any people in the room. _____
   b. There are not many people in the room. _____

4. Two apples
   a. There are not any apples in the bag. _____
   b. There are not many apples in the bag. _____

5. Ten people
   a. There are several people in the car. _____
   b. There are many people in the car. _____

6. Four cars
   a. There are some cars in the parking lot. _____
   b. There are a lot of cars in the parking lot. _____

7. Zero washing machines
   a. There are not any washing machines in the apartment. _____
   b. There are not many washing machines in the apartment. _____

8. Fifty shirts
   a. There are a few shirts in the closet. _____
   b. There are a lot of shirts in the closet. _____

9. Five boxes
   a. There are several boxes on the table. _____
   b. There are many boxes on the table. _____

❷ QUANTIFIERS

Complete the sentences. Use information from the class roster and words from each column.

CLASS ROSTER			
Agustin Aldovar	Venezuela	Muhammad Nur	Egypt
Mehmet Beyoglu	Turkey	Chie Oshima	Japan
Chou-Hsin Chen	China	Christina Paschou	Greece
Teresa Gomez	Mexico	Jaime Rodriguez	Venezuela
Pablo Gonzalez	Venezuela	Jose Sanchez	Venezuela
Jeonghyun Hong	Korea	Alejandro Santiago	Mexico
Su Yuan Huang	China	Laura Sepulveda	Venezuela
Tomohiro Iwasaki	Japan	Sylvia Suarez	Venezuela
Min Jung	Korea	Miyako Tamaki	Japan
Yuko Koyama	Japan	Karina Torrijos	Venezuela
Yong Lee	Korea	Yang Ling Tsu	China
Maria Martinez	Mexico	Keiko Tsukamoto	Japan
Takashi Miki	Japan	So Young	Korea
Mariko Morimoto	Japan		
Margarita Munoz	Mexico		

is	**a**	**student**
are	**any**	**students**
aren't	**a few**	
	many	

1. There _____is_____ _____a_____ ____student____ from Egypt.

2. There _____are_____ ____a few____ ___students___ from Korea.

3. There _____ _____ _____ from Russia.

4. There _____ _____ _____ from Japan.

5. There _____ _____ _____ from Venezuela.

6. There _____ _____ _____ from Turkey.

7. There _____ _____ _____ from Morocco.

8. There _____ _____ _____ from Greece.

(continued on next page)

9. There _____ _____ _____ from Mexico.

10. There _____ _____ _____ from Indonesia.

11. There _____ _____ _____ from China.

12. There _____ _____ _____ from France.

3 QUESTIONS WITH *HOW MANY*

Look at the picture in Exercise 3 on page 103. Write questions. Use **how many**.

1. How many televisions are there?   There are two.

2. _____ There is one.

3. _____ There are three.

4. _____ There are four.

5. _____ There are five.

6. _____ There are six.

7. _____ There are seven.

8. _____ There are eight.

9. _____ There are nine.

10. _____ There are ten.

UNIT

PRESENT AND PRESENT PROGRESSIVE; HOW OFTEN . . . ?; ADVERBS AND EXPRESSIONS OF FREQUENCY

❶ THE SIMPLE PRESENT TENSE AND ADVERBS OF FREQUENCY

Put a check (✓) next to the sentences that are true.

_____ **1.** Americans almost always have dinner after nine o'clock.

_____ **2.** Americans never celebrate birthdays.

_____ **3.** Americans often give a present on a friend's or relative's birthday.

_____ **4.** Americans rarely ski to work.

_____ **5.** Americans always eat rice with dinner.

_____ **6.** There are seldom fireworks on July 4th in the United States.

_____ **7.** Americans don't usually drink tea at five o'clock in the afternoon.

_____ **8.** Thanksgiving is always on a Thursday.

_____ **9.** Americans sometimes work on Sundays.

_____ **10.** Americans don't often drink coffee in the morning.

❷ THE SIMPLE PRESENT TENSE AND ADVERBS OF FREQUENCY

Underline the correct adverbs or expressions of frequency. Then write sentences.

1. The doctor says, "I go to the hospital."

(rarely, <u>usually</u>) <u>I usually go to the hospital.</u>

2. The police officer says, "I arrest people."

(<u>sometimes</u>, never) <u>I sometimes arrest people.</u>

(continued on next page)

111

3. The football player says, "I practice in the middle of the night."

(always, rarely) _____

4. The salesperson says, "I fight with customers."

(always, seldom) _____

5. The taxi driver says, "I drive at night."

(never, often) _____

6. The pharmacist says, "I'm careful."

(always, rarely) _____

7. The mechanic says, "I find the problem with the car."

(almost always, seldom) _____

8. The chef says, "I put lemon in milk."

(never, often) _____

9. The factory worker says, "I'm bored."

(never, once in a while) _____

10. The nurse says, "The hospital is open."

(every day, frequently) _____

11. The firefighter says, "I wear a suit and tie to work."

(every day, almost never) _____

12. The flight attendant says, "We're away from home for three or four days."

(frequently, never) _____

3 QUESTIONS WITH *HOW OFTEN*

Write questions. Use **how often***. Then answer the questions. Use the information in the chart.*

	SWIM	PLAY BASKETBALL	DO EXERCISES	JOG
BARBARA	three times a week	never	every day	rarely
DONNA	once in a while	frequently	four times a week	five days a week
DAVID	never	almost every day	every morning	rarely
ED	once or twice a week	never	never	often
GEORGE	once or twice a week	almost every day	almost every day	almost never

1. (Barbara / do exercises)

   How often does Barbara do exercises?

   She does exercises every day.

2. (Donna / play basketball)

3. (David / swim)

4. (Barbara and Ed / play basketball)

(continued on next page)

5. (Ed / jog)

_____

_____

6. (Barbara / swim)

_____

_____

7. (Barbara and David / jog)

_____

_____

8. (Ed and George / swim)

_____

_____

9. (George and David / play basketball)

_____

_____

10. (George / jog)

_____

_____

11. (you / jog)

_____

_____

12. (you / do exercises)

_____

_____

4 THE SIMPLE PRESENT TENSE

Match the occupations with the activities.

1. __i__ artists
2. _____ bakers
3. _____ bank tellers
4. _____ bus drivers
5. _____ butchers
6. _____ doctors
7. _____ gardeners
8. _____ mechanics
9. _____ newspaper reporters
10. _____ scientists
11. _____ waitresses
12. _____ zookeepers

a. bake bread and cake
b. count money
c. cut meat
d. do experiments
e. drive buses
f. examine patients
g. feed animals
h. fix cars
i. paint pictures
j. serve food
k. water plants and flowers
l. write articles

5 THE SIMPLE PRESENT TENSE VS. THE PRESENT PROGRESSIVE

Complete the sentences. Use the correct form of the verbs in Exercise 4.

1. Scott's a doctor. He _____examines patients_____ every day. Right now he's in his office. He _____is ('s) examining a patient_____.

2. Marilyn's a bus driver. She _____ five days a week. Right now she's at work. She _____.

3. Larry's a mechanic. Every day he _____. Right now he's at his garage. He _____.

4. Anne's a waitress. Every day she _____. Right now she's at the restaurant. She _____.

5. Sandra and Pat are artists. They _____ almost every day. Right now they're both at their studios. They _____.

6. Nicholas and Catherine are scientists. They _____ every day. Right now they're in the lab. They _____.

7. Renée and Cathy are newspaper reporters. They _____ every afternoon. They're at work right now. They _____.

(continued on next page)

8. Arthur's a butcher. He _____ every day. Right now he's

at his store. He _____.

9. Linda's a bank teller. She _____ all day long. Right

now she's at the bank. She _____.

10. Barry and Fred are bakers. They _____ every morning.

They're in the kitchen now. They _____.

11. Ruth's a gardener. She _____ almost every day. Right

now she's at work. She _____.

12. Jeffrey's a zookeeper. He _____ two times a day. Right

now he's in the elephant house. He _____.

6 THE SIMPLE PRESENT TENSE VS. THE PRESENT PROGRESSIVE

Complete the telephone conversation. Use the correct form of the verbs in parentheses.

MARSHA: Hello.

ALAN: Hi, Marsha. This is Alan.

MARSHA: Oh, hi, Alan.

ALAN: What _____*are you doing*_____ right now?
             1. (you / do)

_____ anything important?
        2. (you / do)

MARSHA: No, I _____ some vegetables for dinner. That's all.
                   3. (cut)

ALAN: _____ dinner at this time every evening?
          4. (you / prepare)

MARSHA: Yeah, usually. We _____ at around 8:00. Why? When
                               5. (eat)

_____ dinner?
        6. (you / have)

ALAN: Oh, my family and I _____ much earlier, probably
                              7. (eat)

because our kids _____ to bed by 7:30. In fact, they
                  8. (go)

_____ ready for bed right now.
        9. (get)

MARSHA: Really? Our daughter _____ to bed until 9:30,

10. (not go)

sometimes even ten o'clock. _____ to bed so early on

11. (your kids / go)

the weekends, too?

ALAN: No, but they _____ later than 8:30. They

12. (not stay up)

_____ at around 6:30 every morning, so they

13. (get up)

_____ tired by then. What

14. (be)

_____ all evening? _____ a

15. (your daughter / do)   16. (she / watch)

lot of television?

MARSHA: No, she _____ the violin. Actually, she

17. (practice)

_____ right now.

18. (practice)

ALAN: How often _____?

19. (she / practice)

MARSHA: Every day for at least an hour.

ALAN: You're kidding. _____ well?

20. (she / play)

MARSHA: Very well. We _____ very proud of her.

21. (be)

ALAN: I'm sure. Listen, I _____ on a report for the office, and

22. (work)

there _____ a problem.

23. (be)

_____ a couple of minutes to talk to me about it?

24. (you / have)

MARSHA: Sure.

NON-ACTION VERBS

1 ACTION VERBS VS. NON-ACTION VERBS

Underline the verb in each sentence. Then write **action verb** *or* **non-action verb**.

1. I <u>have</u> a car. _____ non-action verb _____

2. She <u>drives</u> badly. _____ action verb _____

3. I don't have any brothers or sisters. _____

4. Mitchell is having lunch. _____

5. This book belongs to me. _____

6. What do you need? _____

7. Do you like horror movies? _____

8. Do they come by bus every day? _____

9. Do the flowers smell nice? _____

10. Why are you smelling the milk? _____

11. We do a lot of grammar exercises in this class. _____

12. Why does he hate chocolate? _____

13. I don't know the answer. _____

14. Where are they running? _____

2 THE SIMPLE PRESENT TENSE VS. THE PRESENT PROGRESSIVE

Complete the sentences. Circle the correct answers and write them on the lines.

1. I _____ have _____ ten dollars. The money's in my bag.

   a. have

   b. am having

2. We _____ help. Let's ask the teacher.

   a. need

   b. are needing

3. I'm busy. I _____ on the phone.

   a. talk

   b. am talking

4. She _____ it. Explain it to her again.

   a. does not understand

   b. is not understanding

5. Pedro _____ his family. That's why he's sad.

   a. misses

   b. is missing

6. You _____ in the right place. Look over there!

   a. do not look

   b. are not looking

7. There's a problem, but I _____ the answer.

   a. do not know

   b. am not knowing

8. I _____. Don't talk to me!

   a. think

   b. am thinking

(continued on next page)

9. That shirt _____ good. Buy it!

    a. looks

    b. is looking

10. _____ that guy is nice?

    a. Do you think

    b. Are you thinking

11. There's a car outside. _____ to you?

    a. Does it belong

    b. Is it belonging

12. The little boy is unhappy. That's why he _____.

    a. cries

    b. is crying

13. Let's stay. I _____ a good time.

    a. have

    b. am having

14. That music _____ terrible. Turn it off!

    a. sounds

    b. is sounding

3 THE SIMPLE PRESENT TENSE VS. THE PRESENT PROGRESSIVE

Complete the conversation. Write the correct form of the verbs in parentheses. Use contractions if possible.

A: What _____ *do you want* _____ to do now?
              1. (you / want)

B: I _____. _____ to go to the
         2. (not care)   **3. (you / want)**

    movies?

A: What _____?
           4. (play)

B: I _____. I _____ a newspaper.
       5. (not know)   **6. (not have)**

A: Well, let's go for a walk and get one.

B: But it _____.
7. (rain)

A: So what? I _____ an umbrella.
8. (have)

B: But I _____ one.
9. (not have)

A: Well, take mine. I _____ it.
10. (not need)

I _____ the rain.
11. (like)

B: Okay.

A: Maybe Alex _____ to come with us.
12. (want)

B: I _____ so. He _____ a lot of
13. (not think)   14. (have)

homework tonight. He _____ it right now.
15. (do)

A: But I _____ his voice. He _____
16. (hear)   17. (talk)

on the phone.

B: He _____ to a classmate. There's something he
18. (talk)

_____, and he _____ some help.
19. (not understand)   20. (get)

A: How _____?
21. (you / know)

B: I _____ everything.
22. (know)

A: Well, you _____ what's playing at the movies. So let's go!
23. (not know)

UNIT 27

VERBS PLUS NOUNS, GERUNDS, AND INFINITIVES

1 VERBS

Match the sentences with the speakers. (Look at your Student Book if you need help.)

1. __d__ I want to clean the apartment.

2. _____ All of you need to study more.

3. _____ My daughter-in-law does not like to take care of my son.

4. _____ My daughter does not like studying very much.

5. _____ I prefer to wear baggy jeans.

6. _____ I do not enjoy cleaning all the time.

7. _____ I want to speak English perfectly.

8. _____ I'm tired of looking at your pictures.

9. _____ My mother keeps telling me to clean my room.

a. Pete

b. Lulu

c. Doug

d. Yoko

e. Carol

f. Doug

g. Bertha

h. Yoko

i. Norma

❷ GERUNDS

Look at the pictures. Then find the two mistakes in each sentence and correct the mistakes. (Look at the pictures in the Student Book if you need help.)

1. ~~Carol~~ ^{Doug} enjoys to ~~ski~~ ^{skiing}.

2. Pete is good at fix things.

3. Doug enjoys fish.

4. Norma is interested in collect stamps.

5. Lulu enjoys to garden.

6. Yoko is good at to ride horses.

7. Elenore is interested in learn Spanish.

8. Milt is good at cook.

③ VERBS PLUS INFINITIVES AND GERUNDS

Complete the sentences. Write the correct form of the verbs in the box.

be	~~buy~~	help	move	receive
relax	study	swim	study	talk

1. **A:** Why are you going to the store?

   B: I want _____*to buy*_____ some fruit.

2. **A:** Why do you go to the swimming pool on Sunday mornings?

   B: I prefer _____ on Sundays. It's quiet then.

3. **A:** Why are you angry with your roommate?

   B: She never wants _____ with the housework.

4. **A:** Why are you closing the door?

   B: I need _____ to you in private.

5. **A:** Why are Gina and Louis looking for an apartment?

   B: They want _____.

6. **A:** Why are they going to the airport so late?

   B: They do not need _____ at the airport until the evening.

7. **A:** Why do you write so many letters?

   B: Because we like _____ them.

8. **A:** Why do you go to the library after class every day?

   B: I prefer _____ there.

9. **A:** Why do you and your wife always stay home on Sundays?

   B: We like _____.

10. **A:** Why are you putting your books away?

    B: Because I finished _____.

POSSESSIVE ADJECTIVES
AND POSSESSIVE PRONOUNS

 POSSESSIVE PRONOUNS

Write **correct** *if the sentence is correct. Write* **car** *in the sentences where a noun is necessary.*

1. Your is not working. _____Your car is not working._____

2. Mine is not working. _____correct_____

3. Is this yours? _____

4. Ours is over there. _____

5. Please bring me my. _____

6. Where is her? _____

7. Give me hers, please. _____

8. Theirs is on Park Street. _____

9. We need our. _____

10. Their is expensive. _____

11. I like mine a lot. _____

12. Why do you want your? _____

2 POSSESSIVE PRONOUNS

Complete the sentences. Use **mine, yours, his, hers, ours,** *or* **theirs.**

1. That is not her bicycle. _____Hers_____ is blue.

2. That's not my jacket. _____ is gray.

3. **A:** Is that his classroom?

    B: No, _____ is on the fifth floor.

(continued on next page)

4. A: Is that our suitcase?

   B: No, _____ is not light brown. We have a dark brown suitcase.

5. These are not your shoes. _____ are under the bed.

6. A: Is that their house?

   B: No, _____ is on Middle Street.

7. A: Are those your son's sneakers?

   B: No, _____ are a size 12.

8. A: Is that Ms. Gilman's office?

   B: No, _____ is in the next building.

9. These are not Yuri and Natasha's test papers. _____ are on my desk.

10. My roommate and I have a sofa like that one, but _____ is a little bigger.

---

❸ POSSESSIVE ADJECTIVES VS. POSSESSIVE PRONOUNS

Complete the conversations. Use the correct possessive adjective or possessive pronoun.

1. A: This is not _____my_____ coat.

   B: Where's _____yours_____?

   A: In the closet.

2. A: That's _____ ball. Give it to me!

   B: It's not _____. It's _____. It's a birthday present from my brother.

3. A: Whose scarf is this?

   B: It's Nancy's.

   A: Are you sure it's _____? This scarf is green, and she rarely wears green.

   B: I'm sure it's _____.

4. A: We're so happy with _____ new car. We love it.

   B: You're lucky. We don't like _____ at all.

5. A: Do you know Bonnie and Tony Gray? _____ son is on the football team.

   B: We know them, but we don't know _____ son. Our son is on the junior

       high school team, but _____ is on the high school team.

6. A: Is this your husband's hat?

   B: Yes, it is.

   A: How do you know it's _____?

   B: Because all of _____ hats have his name inside.

UNIT

29 REVIEW OF THE SIMPLE PAST TENSE; NEGATIVE QUESTIONS

1 AFFIRMATIVE AND NEGATIVE STATEMENTS WITH THE SIMPLE PAST TENSE

Complete the sentences. Use the affirmative or negative form of the verb in parentheses.

1. Yoko ___*didn't get*___ out of bed
　　　　　　(get)
at six o'clock yesterday.

2. Then she _____
　　　　　　　　　　　　　(make)
breakfast.

3. She _____ for class at
　　　　　　(leave)
half past eight.

4. She and her classmates
_____ all tired.
　　　　(be)

5. She _____
  (have)
lunch alone.

6. In the afternoon she

_____ golf.
  (play)

7. Then she _____
  (buy)
some dog food.

8. Then she _____
  (eat)
dinner with Carol.

9. After dinner she and

Rocky _____
  (watch)

TV.

2 YES / NO QUESTIONS AND SHORT ANSWERS WITH THE SIMPLE PAST TENSE

Answer the questions. Use short answers.

1. Was Carol with her family on Thanksgiving? ___No, she wasn't._____

2. Were your parents born in New York? _____

3. Did you buy anything yesterday? _____

4. Was your father a good student? _____

5. Was it cold yesterday? _____

6. Did you take a shower yesterday? _____

7. Were you born in a hospital? _____

(continued on next page)

8. Did your parents get married five years ago? _____

9. Did you and a friend go to the movies last night? _____

10. Was the last grammar exercise easy? _____

11. Did your English teacher give you a test last week? _____

12. Were you absent from your last English class? _____

❸ YES / NO QUESTIONS AND SHORT ANSWERS WITH THE PAST TENSE OF *BE*

Write questions and answers. Use the past tense of **be**.

1. **A:** We had a nice holiday.

   B: _Were you with your whole family?_ (you / with your whole family)

   A: _No, my daughter was in Montreal._ (no / my daughter / in Montreal)

2. **A:** I bought these new shoes yesterday.

   B: _____ (they / on sale)

   A: _____ (yes / they / only $25)

3. **A:** _____ (you / at home / last night)

   B: _____ (no / I / at the library)

4. **A:** _____ (the guests / late for the party)

   B: _____ (no / they / all on time)

5. **A:** _____ (it / warm / in Australia)

   B: _____ (the weather / beautiful / every day)

6. **A:** _____ (the movie / good)

   B: _____ (it / okay)

7. **A:** _____ (the people at the party / friendly)

   B: _____ (most of them / very nice)

8. **A:** I called the lawyer.

   B: _____ (he / there)

   A: _____ (no / he / in a meeting)

4 NEGATIVE QUESTIONS

Complete the conversations with negative questions. Use the verbs in parentheses.

1. **A:** I'm so upset. I think I failed my math test.

   B: _____Didn't you study_____ for it?
   (study)
   A: Yeah, but it was really difficult.

2. **A:** I'm really hungry.

   B: _____ breakfast?
   (eat)
   A: No, I didn't have time.

3. **A:** What's the homework for tomorrow?

   B: _____ in class yesterday?
   (be)
   A: Yeah, but I didn't write down the homework.

4. **A:** Hi, honey. How's the weather there?

   B: It's raining.

   A: _____ yesterday?
   (rain)
   B: It rains almost everyday here.

5. **A:** I don't want to go to the Italian restaurant again.

   B: _____ it the last time we went there?
   (like)
   A: Yeah, but we go there so much. I'm tired of the place.

6. **A:** I was home yesterday morning at nine.

   B: _____ your history class at nine?
   (be)
   A: I didn't go.

7. **A:** What movie do you want to see?

   B: Why don't we go to *The Lost Island*?

   A: _____ that with Eddie a couple of weeks ago?
   (see)
   B: Yeah, but it was really good. I'd like to see it again.

WH- QUESTIONS IN THE SIMPLE PAST TENSE

1 **WH- QUESTIONS IN THE SIMPLE PAST TENSE**

Complete the conversations. Circle the correct questions and write them on the lines.

1. A: I was absent yesterday.

   B: _____What was wrong?_____

   a. Who was absent?   **(b.)** What was wrong?

   A: I was ill.

2. A: We had dinner at the new Mexican restaurant.

   B: _____

   a. How was the food?   **b.** Did you like the food?

   A: Yes. It was very good.

3. A: You forgot Cathy's birthday.

   B: _____

   a. When was it?   **b.** Where was she?

   A: Last Thursday.

4. A: I went to bed at eight o'clock last night.

   B: _____

   a. What did you do?   **b.** Why were you so tired?

   A: I don't know. I didn't feel very well.

5. A: You missed a great party.

   B: _____

   a. Who was there?   **b.** How was the party?

   A: People from our class and their friends.

6. A: I found your keys.

B: _____

    a. Where did you find them?   **b.** Why were they there?

A: Under the desk.

7. A: I got everything right on the test.

B: _____

    a. Really? Where were the answers to the first and third questions?

    b. Really? What were the answers to the first and third questions?

A: The answer to the first was C, and D was the answer to the third.

8. A: We were on vacation for two weeks.

B: _____

    a. Where did you go?   **b.** How was it?

A: It was great.

9. A: We had a great time in Hong Kong.

B: _____

    a. Who were you with?   **b.** When did you go there?

A: We were there about two years ago.

10. A: I went to a great movie with Andrea last night.

B: _____

    a. Why didn't you call me and see if I wanted to go?

    b. Why did you go with Andrea and not me?

A: I did, but you weren't home.

2 WH- QUESTIONS IN THE SIMPLE PAST TENSE

Complete the questions. Use **was**, **were**, *or* **did**. *Then match the questions and answers.*

_e_ **1.** Why ____did____ you go there?

____ **2.** Who _____ you with?

____ **3.** What _____ you wear?

____ **4.** How _____ the weather?

____ **5.** Where _____ you yesterday?

____ **6.** How _____ you get to the beach?

____ **7.** Where _____ your husband?

____ **8.** When _____ he come home?

____ **9.** What _____ the problem with the bus?

____ **10.** Why _____ he angry?

____ **11.** Where _____ your friends meet you?

____ **12.** Why _____ your friends late?

a. At the beach.

b. It was sunny and warm.

c. By bus.

d. It was crowded.

e. We wanted to swim.

f. Some friends.

g. At the bus station.

h. They woke up late.

i. My new bathing suit.

j. At his office.

k. He didn't go to the beach with us.

l. Late last night.

3 WH- QUESTIONS WITH THE PAST TENSE OF *BE*

Complete the conversations. Write correct questions.

1. A: Did you pay a lot of money for those sunglasses?

   B: No, they were on sale.

   A: When __were they on sale_____?

   B: Last week.

2. A: I tried to call you last night.

   B: I wasn't home.

   A: Where _____?

   B: At a friend's apartment.

3. A: Did you have your history test yesterday?

   B: No, we had it today.

   A: How _____?

   B: It was okay, but I didn't know the answers to two of the questions.

4. **A:** Did the kids go swimming?

   B: No, they were afraid.

   A: Why _____?

   B: The water was deep.

5. **A:** Did you go to the basketball game?

   B: Yeah, it was a great game.

   A: What _____?

   B: I don't remember the score, but our team won.

6. **A:** Those are beautiful shoes. Where did you get them?

   B: At a store on Washington Street.

   A: What _____?

   B: I think the name of the store was Dalton's. Or, was it Dillon's?

7. **A:** Did your dog have her puppies yet?

   B: She sure did—six of them.

   A: When _____?

   B: They were born a few days ago.

8. **A:** What's new?

   B: The police were here.

   A: Why _____?

   B: Someone called them, but I don't know why.

9. **A:** You were brave to go there alone.

   B: I wasn't alone.

   A: Who _____?

   B: My brother and sister.

10. **A:** Did you ever read this book?

    B: Yes, it was about Eleanor Roosevelt.

    A: Who _____?

    B: She was the wife of President Roosevelt.

BE GOING TO FOR THE FUTURE; FUTURE AND PAST TIME MARKERS

1 FUTURE TIME MARKERS

*Rewrite the sentences. Replace the underlined words with another future time expression. Use **tonight** or combine the correct words from each column.*

	week
next	month
this	morning
tomorrow	afternoon
	night
	evening

(It's eleven o'clock in the morning on Wednesday, July 3rd.)

1. Keith is going to attend a meeting <u>in four hours</u>.

   Keith is going to attend a meeting this afternoon.

2. Keith and his girlfriend, Andrea, are going to visit a friend in the hospital in <u>eight hours</u>.

   _____

3. Andrea is going to go on vacation <u>in one month</u>.

   _____

4. Keith and his brother are going to play tennis <u>in twenty hours</u>.

   _____

5. Keith's brother is going to see the doctor <u>in one week</u>.

   _____

6. Keith is going to call his mother <u>in eleven hours</u>.

_____

7. Keith and Andrea are going to go to the movies <u>in thirty-four hours</u>.

_____

❷ FUTURE TIME MARKERS

Rewrite the sentences. Replace the underlined words with another future time expression. Use **in**.

(It is ten o'clock in the morning on Friday, March 5th.)

1. Richard is going to have lunch <u>at two o'clock this afternoon</u>.

Richard is going to have lunch in four hours.

2. Richard and Irene are going to see his parents <u>on March 19th</u>.

_____

3. Irene is going to get a haircut <u>on Monday, March 8th</u>.

_____

4. Richard is going to graduate from college <u>on May 5th</u>.

_____

5. Irene is going to arrive at Richard's house <u>at 10:10 this morning</u>.

_____

❸ FUTURE PLANS

What are your plans for tomorrow? Put a check (✓) next to the things you are probably going to do. Put an **X** *next to the things you are definitely not going to do.*

_____ **1.** study

_____ **2.** go shopping

_____ **3.** take pictures

_____ **4.** watch TV

_____ **5.** go out with friends

_____ **6.** listen to music

_____ **7.** visit relatives

_____ **8.** talk on the telephone

_____ **9.** take a shower

_____ **10.** write a letter

_____ **11.** go skiing

_____ **12.** stay home

4 AFFIRMATIVE AND NEGATIVE STATEMENTS WITH *BE GOING TO*

Write six true sentences about your plans for tomorrow. Use the information from Exercise 3.

Example: __✓__ study   __X__ write a letter

    I am going to study tomorrow. _____

    I am not going to write a letter. _____

1. _____

2. _____

3. _____

4. _____

5. _____

6. _____

5 AFFIRMATIVE STATEMENTS WITH *BE GOING TO*

Some people are going out. What are they going to do? Make guesses and write sentences with **be going to**.

Nina is taking a tennis racket and a textbook.

1.   She's going to play tennis. _____

2. _____

Mr. and Mrs. Wu are taking paper and envelopes and skis.

3. _____

4. _____

Richard is taking CDs and a camera.

5. _____

6. _____

❻ NEGATIVE STATEMENTS WITH *BE GOING TO*

Write sentences about the future. Use **not** *and* **be going to***.*

1. It's Wednesday morning. Reggie usually plays tennis on Wednesday afternoon, but he has a bad cold.

   _He isn't going to play_____ tennis this afternoon.

2. It's July. Joan usually takes a vacation in August, but she has money problems this year.

   _____ a vacation this August.

3. Mary always takes a shower in the morning, but there's no hot water today.

   _____ a shower this morning.

4. It's eleven o'clock in the morning. The children usually play outside after lunch, but the weather is terrible today.

   _____ outside this afternoon.

5. It's six o'clock. Carl and his wife usually watch television after dinner, but there's nothing good on television.

   _____ television tonight.

6. It's eleven o'clock. I usually eat lunch around noon, but I finished a big breakfast at 10:30.

   _____ lunch at noon today.

7. It's twelve noon. My friend and I like to swim on Saturday afternoons, but my friend went away for the weekend and I'm tired.

   _____ this afternoon.

8. It's nine o'clock in the morning. Dr. Morita usually sees patients at his office every morning, but there's an emergency at the hospital. He can't leave until noon.

   _____ patients at his office this morning.

9. I usually wake up at six o'clock in the morning, but tomorrow is a holiday.

   _____ at six o'clock tomorrow morning.

10. It's ten o'clock in the morning. The letter carrier usually delivers all the mail by one o'clock, but he started late this morning.

    _____ all the mail by one o'clock today.

❼ WH- QUESTIONS WITH *BE GOING TO*

Write questions. Use **be going to**.

1. What / he / make

   <u>What is he going to make?</u>

2. Who / cook / tonight

   _____

3. When / dinner / be / ready

   _____

4. Why / he / cook / so much food

   _____

5. How long / he / need / to cook the dinner

   _____

6. Who / come

   _____

7. How / he / cook / the lamb

   _____

8. Where / all of your guests / sit

   _____

9. What / you / do

   _____

10. How long / your guests / stay

    _____

8 WH- QUESTIONS WITH BE GOING TO

Write the correct questions from Exercise 7.

1. **A:** __Who's going to cook tonight?__

   B: My husband.

2. **A:** _____

   B: Soup, salad, lamb, potatoes, some vegetables, and dessert.

3. **A:** _____

   B: We're going to have a dinner party.

4. **A:** _____

   B: He's going to roast it in the oven.

5. **A:** _____

   B: About fifteen of my relatives.

6. **A:** _____

   B: My husband's fast. Probably two or three hours.

7. **A:** _____

   B: I'm going to wash the dishes.

8. **A:** _____

   B: At around seven o'clock.

9. **A:** _____

   B: They're going to come at 6:00 and probably stay until about 11:00.

10. **A:** _____

    B: My sister's going to bring extra chairs.

❾ PRESENT PROGRESSIVE FOR NOW AND FOR FUTURE

Underline the verb in each sentence. Write **now** *if the speaker is talking about now. Write* **future** *if the speaker is talking about the future.*

1. What <u>are</u> you <u>doing</u> tomorrow morning? _____ future

2. What <u>are</u> you <u>doing</u>? _____ now

3. I'm doing a grammar exercise. _____

4. We're not going on vacation in July. _____

5. She's leaving in two hours. _____

6. Are you doing anything special? _____

7. Is the plumber coming soon? _____

8. The students are not listening. _____

9. Where are you going this weekend? _____

10. Why is he waiting? _____

❿ PRESENT PROGRESSIVE FOR FUTURE

Roger and Helen are taking a trip to Great Britain. Here is their schedule. Write sentences. Use the present progressive.

May 8	6:00 P.M. 7:30	Meet your group at the airport Fly to London
May 9	6:45 A.M.	Arrive in London
May 9 and 10		Stay at the London Regency Hotel
May 9	2:00 P.M. 4:30 7:30	Visit Buckingham Palace Have tea at the Ritz Hotel Go to the theater
May 10	9:00 A.M. 12:00 P.M.	Go on a tour of central London Eat lunch at a typical English pub
May 11	8:00 A.M.	Leave for Scotland

1.   They are meeting their group at the airport at 6:00 p.m. on May 8.

2. _____

3. _____

4. _____

5. _____

6. _____

7. _____

8. _____

9. _____

10. _____

11   YES / NO QUESTIONS AND ANSWERS WITH THE PRESENT PROGRESSIVE FOR FUTURE

Write questions. Use the present progressive. Then answer them. Use short answers.

1. you / go / to English class / tomorrow

     Are you going to English class tomorrow?   Yes, I am. (OR: No, I'm not.)

2. you / go / to the movies / this weekend

   _____   _____

3. you / take a trip / next week

   _____   _____

4. your friend / leave / in two hours

   _____   _____

5. your classmates / meet you / tonight

   _____   _____

6. your mother / drive to work / tomorrow

   _____   _____

7. your father / take an English class / next year

   _____   _____

(continued on next page)

8. your neighbors / do anything / this weekend

_____   _____

9. you and your friends / play cards / next Saturday

_____   _____

10. your parents / call / your teacher / tonight

_____   _____

12 *WH-* QUESTIONS WITH THE PRESENT PROGRESSIVE FOR FUTURE

Ask Rosemary about her vacation plans. Write questions. Use a word from each column and the present progressive.

Why		stay
When		take
Where		go
Who	you	go with
How long		leave
What		drive
How		get there

1. Where are you going? _____

To Colorado.

2. _____

On September 16th.

3. _____

By car.

4. _____

Airplane tickets are too expensive.

5. _____

Two weeks.

6. _____

Some friends from college.

7. _____

A tent, sleeping bags, and bikes.

WILL FOR THE FUTURE

 1 AFFIRMATIVE STATEMENTS WITH *WILL*

Complete the conversations. Use **I'll** *and the words in the box.*

buy you some	make you a sandwich	wash them
get you some water	~~close the window~~	drive you
turn on the air conditioner	get you some aspirin	help you

1. A: I'm cold.

   B: <u> I'll close the window. </u>

2. A: I'm thirsty.

   B: _____

3. A: I can't lift this box.

   B: _____

4. A: I need some stamps.

   B: _____

5. A: I'm hot.

   B: _____

6. A: I'm hungry.

   B: _____

7. A: I have a headache.

   B: _____

8. A: I'm late for class.

   B: _____

9. A: There are dirty dishes in the sink.

   B: _____

2 CONTRACTIONS WITH *WILL*

Write the sentences with contractions.

1. We will meet you at 8:00. _____We'll meet you at 8:00._____

2. He will not lose his job. _____

3. I will have a cup of coffee. _____

4. It will rain this evening. _____

5. She will not be happy. _____

6. They will have a good time. _____

7. You will not like it. _____

3 WILL VS. *BE GOING TO* VS. PRESENT PROGRESSIVE FOR FUTURE

Complete the sentences. Circle the correct words and write them on the lines.

1. **A:** What's the weather forecast for tomorrow?

   B: The newspaper says it _____will snow_____.

   a. is snowing   **b.** will snow

2. **A:** Where are you going with the soap and water?

   B: I _____ wash the car.

   a. am going to   **b.** will

3. **A:** Do you see my umbrella?

   B: Yes, it's over there. I _____ get it for you.

   a. am going to   **b.** will

4. **A:** Why is Myra so happy these days?

   B: She _____ get married.

   a. is going to   **b.** will

5. **A:** Why _____ see that film?

   a. are you going to   **b.** will you

   B: I heard it was good.

6. A: The dishwasher isn't working. I'm going to call the repairman.

   B: No, don't. I _____ it.

     a. am fixing   **b.** will fix

7. A: I think men _____ dresses in the future.

     a. are wearing   **b.** will wear

   B: You're crazy!

8. A: _____ anything this weekend?

     a. Are you doing   **b.** Will you do

   B: I'm not sure yet. Why?

9. A: _____ everything by computer in fifty years?

     a. Are people buying   **b.** Will people buy

   B: Maybe.

4 NEGATIVE STATEMENTS WITH *WILL*

Write negative sentences with the same meaning.

1. The car will be small.

   The car won't be big.

2. I'll leave early.

   _____

3. It'll be cold.

   _____

4. Coffee will cost less.

   _____

5. The dishes will be clean.

   _____

(continued on next page)

6. We will come after seven o'clock.

_____

7. Mr. and Mrs. McNamara will buy an old car.

_____

8. I'll make a few eggs.

_____

9. Valerie will win the game.

_____

10. The parking lot will be empty.

_____

5 **AFFIRMATIVE AND NEGATIVE STATEMENTS AND *YES / NO* AND *WH-* QUESTIONS WITH *WILL***

*A fortune teller is telling Mark about his future. Complete the conversation. Use **will** or **won't** and the words in parentheses.*

FORTUNE TELLER: Your future _____ will be _____ a happy one.
                                              1. (be)

MARK: _____ rich?
          2. (I / be)

FORTUNE TELLER: Yes. You _____ a very rich woman.
                              3. (marry)

MARK: Where _____ her?
                4. (I / meet)

FORTUNE TELLER: That I can't tell you, but it _____ love at first
                                                   5. (be)

sight.

MARK: _____ me forever?
          6. (she / love)

FORTUNE TELLER: Forever.

MARK: When _____?
               7. (we / meet)

FORTUNE TELLER: Soon.

MARK: What about children?

FORTUNE TELLER: You _____ many children—just two, a boy
                        8. (not have)

and a girl.

MARK: That's a good number. What else?

FORTUNE TELLER: You _____ famous.
                                                    9. (be)

MARK: Really? Why _____ famous?
                                    10. (I / be)

FORTUNE TELLER: I'm not sure, but it _____ fun for you.
                                                            11. (not be)

People _____ you all the time.
                            12. (bother)

MARK: Oh! I _____ that.
                                13. (not like)

_____ everything?
                14. (our home / have)

FORTUNE TELLER: Yes, everything.

MARK: Good. Then we _____ it, and
                                        15. (not leave)

people _____ us.
                    16. (not bother)

FORTUNE TELLER: But then you _____ a prisoner in you own
                                                17. (become)

home. _____ you happy?
            18. (that / make)

MARK: Oh, why isn't life perfect?

FORTUNE TELLER: That I cannot tell you.

UNIT

33 COUNT AND NON-COUNT NOUNS AND QUANTIFIERS

1 COUNT NOUNS VS. NON-COUNT NOUNS

Look at the store signs. Write the correct aisle number.

1	4	7
Eggs Butter Juice Cheese Milk	Toilet Paper Paper Towels Napkins Plastic Bags	Frozen Food Ice Cream

2	5	8
Bread Rolls	Potato Chips Cookies Cereal	Canned Vegetables Canned Fish Rice

3	6	9
Toothbrushes Toothpaste Soap Shampoo	Sugar Flour Salt	Fresh Fruit

1. <u>Sugar</u> is in aisle _6_.

2. <u>Cookies</u> are in aisle ____.

3. <u>Ice cream</u> is in aisle ____.

4. <u>Eggs</u> are in aisle ____.

5. <u>Fruit</u> is in aisle ____.

6. Canned <u>vegetables</u> are in aisle ____.

7. <u>Napkins</u> are in aisle ____.

8. <u>Milk</u> is in aisle ____.

9. <u>Rice</u> is in aisle ____.

10. Plastic <u>bags</u> are in aisle ____.

11. <u>Potato chips</u> are in aisle ____.

12. Frozen <u>food</u> is in aisle ____.

13. <u>Bread</u> is in aisle ____.

14. Canned <u>fish</u> is in aisle ____.

15. <u>Toothbrushes</u> are in aisle ____.

2 COUNT NOUNS VS. NON-COUNT NOUNS

Write the underlined words in Exercise 1 in the correct column.

Count Nouns	Non-Count Nouns
cookies	sugar

3 COUNT NOUNS VS. NON-COUNT NOUNS

*Circle the twelve words that don't belong in the lists of count nouns and non-count nouns. Then write correct lists. Write **a**, **an**, or **some** before each word.*

Count Nouns	Non-Count Nouns	Count Nouns	Non-Count Nouns
egg	books	an egg	some bread
bread	food	some books	some food
furniture	water		
student	people		
money	paper		
information	uncle		
teeth	homework		
rain	advice		
children	television		
friends	traffic		
oil	questions		
animal	computer		

4 COUNT NOUNS VS. NON-COUNT NOUNS

Complete the sentences. Circle the correct answers and write them on the lines.

1. Do you have _____ a pencil _____?

   a. some pencil

   (b.) a pencil

2. The _____ on the table.

   a. money is

   b. money are

3. There _____ in the refrigerator.

   a. is some milk

   b. are some milks

4. We don't have _____.

   a. much book

   b. many books

5. Do you want _____?

   a. a magazine

   b. some magazine

6. I'm sorry I'm late. The _____ terrible.

   a. traffic was

   b. traffics were

7. Do you like Chinese _____?

   a. food

   b. foods

8. Do you have _____?

   a. a water

   b. any water

9. Is there _____ in the bedroom?

    a. a radio

    b. any radio

10. Don't rush! We have a lot of _____.

    a. time

    b. times

11. I want _____.

    a. an information

    b. some information

5 A VS. *THE*

Complete the conversations. Use **a** *or* **the**.

1. A: _____The_____ food is very good.

    B: Thanks. There's more in _____the_____ kitchen.

2. A: What would you like to drink?

    B: _____ cup of coffee, please.

3. A: How did you get here?

    B: I took _____ subway.

4. A: What are you doing?

    B: I'm listening to _____ radio.

5. A: Do you have _____ car?

    B: No, but I'd like to buy one.

6. A: What is _____ capital of the United States?

    B: Washington, D.C. It's _____ pretty big city.

7. A: How did you do on _____ test?

    B: Okay, but I wasn't sure about _____ last part.

8. A: Look! Here's _____ postcard from Suzanne.

    B: That's _____ beautiful picture. Where is she?

6 SOME VS. ANY VS. A

*Jack went shopping. He didn't buy everything on his shopping list, but he crossed out the things he bought. Write sentences about what he did and didn't buy. Use **some**, **any**, or **a**.*

Shopping List

~~Bananas~~	Toothbrush
Cheese	~~Potatoes~~
~~Orange juice~~	Lettuce
Lemons	Carrots
~~Newspaper~~	~~Butter~~
Bread	~~Milk~~
Onions	~~Eggs~~

1. He bought some bananas.

2. He didn't buy any cheese.

3. _____

4. _____

5. _____

6. _____

7. _____

8. _____

9. _____

10. _____

11. _____

12. _____

13. _____

14. _____

7 COUNT AND NON-COUNT NOUN QUANTIFIERS

Write true sentences. Choose words from each column.

I have	a lot of a little a few	cheese in my pocket food in my refrigerator money in my pocket books next to my bed shirts in my closet
I don't have	much many any	friends free time children work to do today questions for my teacher jewelry medicine in my bathroom problems with English grammar photographs in my wallet ice cream at home

1. I don't have any cheese in my pocket.

2.

3.

4.

5.

6.

7.

8.

9.

10.

34 QUESTIONS WITH ANY / SOME / HOW MUCH / HOW MANY; QUANTIFIERS; CONTAINERS

1 CONTAINERS AND NON-COUNT NOUNS

Match the containers and non-count nouns.

_b_	**1.** a can of	**a.**	lettuce
____	**2.** a carton of	**b.**	soda
____	**3.** a head of	**c.**	bread
____	**4.** a loaf of	**d.**	milk

Do the same with these words.

____	**5.** a bottle of	**e.**	cake
____	**6.** a box of	**f.**	cigarettes
____	**7.** a pack of	**g.**	juice
____	**8.** a piece of	**h.**	cereal

Do the same with these words, too.

____	**9.** a bar of	**i.**	toothpaste
____	**10.** a jar of	**j.**	toilet paper
____	**11.** a roll of	**k.**	jam
____	**12.** a tube of	**l.**	soap

② QUESTIONS WITH *HOW MUCH* AND *HOW MANY* AND CONTAINERS

Look at Tina's cash register receipt and answer the questions.

```
6 Soda            $2.19
1 Bread           $1.05
1 Milk            $1.19
2 Lettuce         $3.58
3 Apple juice     $5.40
1 Cereal          $2.29
4 Toilet paper    $1.69
3 Soap            $2.45
1 Toothpaste      $2.39
2 Jam             $3.38
         TOTAL   $25.61


THANK YOU FOR SHOPPING
      AT CASTLE'S
```

1. How much soda did she buy?

   Six cans.

2. How many loaves of bread did she buy?

   One.

3. How much milk did she buy?

   _____

4. How much lettuce did she buy?

   _____

5. How many bottles of apple juice did she buy? _____

6. How many boxes of cereal did she buy?

   _____

7. How much toilet paper did she buy?

   _____

8. How much soap did she buy?

   _____

9. How much toothpaste did she buy?

   _____

10. How many jars of jam did she buy?

   _____

❸ YES / NO QUESTIONS WITH COUNT AND NON-COUNT NOUNS

*Write questions. Use **a**, **an**, or **any**. Then answer the questions with short answers.*

1. telephone / in your bedroom

   <u>Is there a telephone in your bedroom?</u>   Yes, there is. (OR: No, there isn't.)

2. plants / in your home

   <u>Are there any plants in your home?</u>   Yes, there is. (OR: No, there isn't.)

3. trash / in your kitchen

   <u>Is there any trash in your kitchen?</u>   Yes, there is. (OR: No, there isn't.)

4. furniture / in your home

5. clothes / in your closet

6. money / under your bed

7. alarm clock / next to your bed

8. snow / outside your home

9. sink / in your bathroom

10. dishes / in your kitchen sink

11. pictures / in your bedroom

12. candy / in your home

13. window / in your kitchen

_____　_____

14. television / in your living room

_____　_____

4 QUESTIONS WITH *HOW MUCH* AND *HOW MANY*

Complete the conversation. Write questions using **how much** *or* **how many**.

A: Are you going to the store?

B: Yes, why?

A: I need some things. I need some cheese.

B:　How much cheese do you need? _____
　　　　　　　　　　　　　　　1.

A: About a pound. And I want some eggs.

B:　How many eggs do you want? _____
　　　　　　　　　　　　　　　2.

A: A dozen. I also need some flour.

B: _____
　　　　　　　　　　　　　　　3.

A: One pound, I think.

B: Do you want any sugar?

A: No, I have sugar.

B: _____
　　　　　　　　　　　　　　　4.

A: I have a few cups, at least. But I want some bananas.

B: _____
　　　　　　　　　　　　　　　5.

A: Five or six. I want some oranges, too.

B: _____
　　　　　　　　　　　　　　　6.

A: A few. Oh, and I need some cereal.

B: _____
　　　　　　　　　　　　　　　7.

(continued on next page)

A: Just one box. I also need some potatoes.

B: _____
8.

A: Get about ten. Oh, one more thing. I want some milk.

B: _____
9.

A: Half a gallon. Oh, don't forget to get some flowers. I want roses.

B: _____
10.

A: Half a dozen.

B: Is that it? Are you sure you don't want any cookies?

A: No, I have enough cookies.

B: _____
11.

A: Two dozen. Here, let me give you some money.

B: I have money.

A: _____
12.

B: About twenty dollars.

A: Here. Take another twenty.

5 TOO MUCH, TOO MANY, AND *NOT ENOUGH*

Write sentences about the pictures. Use **too much**, **too many**, *or* **not enough** *and the words in the box.*

air	birds	days	furniture	~~people~~	toothpaste
batteries	chairs	food	numbers	shampoo	water

1.

There are too many

people in the boat.

2.

_____

_____

3.

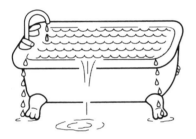

_____

_____

4.

_____

_____

5.

_____

_____

6.

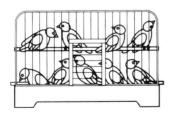

_____

_____

7.

_____

_____

8.

_____

_____

9.

_____

_____

(continued on next page)

10.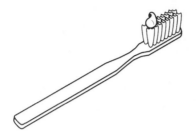

11.

12.

_____

_____

6 TOO LITTLE AND TOO FEW

Rewrite the sentences. Use **too little** *or* **too few**.

1. We don't have enough chairs.

  We have too few chairs. _____

2. There isn't enough salt in this soup.

  There's too little salt in this soup. _____

3. There weren't enough people for two teams.

  _____

4. We didn't have enough paper for everyone in the class.

  _____

5. There wasn't enough food for fifteen people.

  _____

6. You don't have enough information.

  _____

7. There aren't enough bedrooms in that apartment.

  _____

8. We didn't have enough time for the test.

  _____

9. These aren't enough bananas for a banana cake.

_____

10. There aren't enough sales clerks at that store.

_____

7 REVIEW OF QUANTIFIERS

Complete the sentences. Circle the correct answers and write them on the lines.

1. What did the student say to the teacher?

"I didn't finish the homework. I _____didn't have enough_____ time."

   a. had too much

   (b.) didn't have enough

2. What did the driver say to the passenger?

"We _____ gas. We need to go to the gas station."

   a. have too much

   b. don't have enough

3. What did the passenger say to the driver?

"There _____ cars. Let's go to another parking lot."

   a. are too many

   b. aren't enough

4. What did the cashier say to the child?

"I'm sorry. You have _____ money. Go home and get some

more."

   a. too much

   b. too little

(continued on next page)

5. Ted and Niki wanted to see a movie, but there was a long line for tickets. What did Ted say?

   "There are _____ people. Let's see another movie."

   a. too many

   b. too few

6. What did the doctor say to the patient?

   "You said you're on a diet, but you lost only one pound last month. That _____ weight."

   a. is too much

   b. isn't enough

7. What did the photography teacher say to the student?

   "This picture is dark. You had _____ light."

   a. too much

   b. too little

8. What did Mitchell's mother say to him?

   "You ate _____ fruit. That's why you have a stomachache."

   a. too much

   b. too little

9. What did the customer say to the waitress?

   "There are _____ forks on the table for six people. Please bring some more."

   a. too many

   b. too few

10. What did Debbie say to her roommate?

    "You bought _____ juice. There's no place to put all these bottles."

    a. too much

    b. too little

CAN AND *COULD* FOR ABILITY AND POSSIBILITY; *MAY I, CAN I,* AND *COULD I* FOR POLITE REQUESTS

 ABILITY

Look at the job advertisements. Look at the qualifications of Martha, Frank, Les, and Rosa. Then answer the questions.

WANTED
SECRETARY
Type 70 words per minute.
Need to speak Spanish.

WANTED
SUMMER BABYSITTER
Take two small children to the beach every day. Also, go horseback riding with ten-year-old girl.

DRIVER WANTED
Drive truck to airport every day. Pick up boxes and deliver to downtown offices.

WANTED
SUMMER CAMP WORKER
◆ Teach children the guitar
◆ Also work with children in art class

	Martha	Frank	Les	Rosa
draw	no	no	yes	yes
drive	yes	no	yes	no
lift 100 pounds	no	no	yes	yes
play the guitar	no	yes	no	yes
ride a horse	yes	no	no	no
speak Spanish	no	yes	no	yes
swim	yes	yes	no	yes
type	yes	yes	no	no

1. Which job is good for Martha? The job as a _____summer babysitter_____ .

2. Which job is good for Frank? The job as a _____ .

3. Which job is good for Les? The job as a _____ .

4. Which job is good for Rosa? The job as a _____ .

2 AFFIRMATIVE AND NEGATIVE STATEMENTS WITH *CAN* FOR ABILITY

Look at the information in Exercise 1 again. Then answer the questions.
Use **can** *or* **can't**.

1. Why is the job as babysitter good for Martha?

   She ___can swim and ride a horse._____

2. Why isn't the job as babysitter good for Rosa?

   She ___can swim, but she can't ride a horse._____

3. Why isn't the job as babysitter good for Les?

   He ___can't swim, and he can't ride a horse._____

4. Why is the job as driver good for Les?

   He _____

5. Why is the job as secretary good for Frank?

   He _____

6. Why is the job as summer camp worker good for Rosa?

   She _____

7. Why isn't the job as driver good for Frank?

   He _____

8. Why isn't the job as secretary good for Martha?

   She _____

9. Why isn't the job as driver good for Rosa?

   She _____

10. Why isn't the job as summer camp worker good for Les?

    He _____

11. Why isn't the job as summer camp worker good for Martha?

    She _____

12. Why isn't the job as secretary good for Les?

    He _____

3 **YES / NO QUESTIONS WITH CAN**

Write questions. Use **can**. *Then answer the questions. Use short answers.*

1. you / drive

Can you drive?   Yes, I can. (OR: No, I can't.)

2. your mother / lift 100 pounds

3. your father / play the guitar

4. your best friend / ride a horse

5. your parents / speak Spanish

6. you / swim

7. you / type

4 **AFFIRMATIVE AND NEGATIVE STATEMENTS WITH COULD FOR PAST ABILITY**

Complete the sentences. Use **could** *or* **couldn't** *and the verbs in parentheses.*

1. I'm sorry that I _____couldn't call_____ you yesterday. I was very busy.
                    (call)

2. We enjoyed our holiday in Spain because we _____ our
                                        (practice)
Spanish.

3. We (go) _____ to the party last night. Our son was ill.
              (go)

4. I didn't answer the questions. I _____ the story.
                          (understand)

(continued on next page)

5. I had a terrible stomachache yesterday. I _____ a thing.
   (eat)

6. In high school I had a lot of free time. I _____ soccer with
   (play)

   my friends every Saturday and Sunday.

7. We didn't meet our friends for dinner last night. We _____
   (find)

   the restaurant.

8. Our room in that hotel was terrible. We _____ the people in
   (hear)

   the other rooms all the time.

9. Last weekend, we stayed indoors. It was very cold, and we _____
   (go)

   outside.

10. I liked my summer vacation. I _____ whatever I wanted.
    (do)

⑤ MAY AND CAN FOR POLITE REQUESTS

Make polite requests. Use **may I** *or* **can I**.

1. You have a doctor's appointment at four o'clock. You want to leave early because class
   finishes at four o'clock. Ask your teacher.

   __Can I leave class early? (OR: May I leave class early?)__

2. You're in a friend's room. You're hot and you want to open the window. Ask your friend.

   _____

3. You're in an office. You want to use the telephone on the secretary's desk. Ask the
   secretary.

   _____

4. Your classmate has a car, but you don't have one. It's raining, and you want to get a
   ride. Ask your classmate.

   _____

5. You made a mistake. You don't have an eraser, but your classmate has an eraser. Ask
   your classmate.

   _____

6. You're at your neighbor's house. You want to have a drink of water. Ask your neighbor.

_____

7. You have a question about something in your grammar book. Ask your teacher.

_____

8. You're at a restaurant. You want to sit at the empty table in the corner. Ask the waiter.

_____

MAY OR *MIGHT* FOR POSSIBILITY

1 *MAY* FOR PERMISSION AND POSSIBILITY

Write **permission** *if the speaker is giving, refusing, or asking for permission. Write* **possibility** *if the speaker is talking about possibility.*

1. Don't call Carol. She may be asleep.   *possibility*

2. It's noisy outside. May I close the window?   *permission*

3. You may not talk during the test.   _____

4. The government may raise taxes.   _____

5. Lie down. You may feel better.   _____

6. You may enter that room of the old house, but be careful.   _____

7. Some of the students may not do the homework.   _____

8. May my roommate come to the party, too?   _____

9. The mailman is coming. There may be a letter for me. _____

10. Nobody may leave before eleven o'clock.   _____

2 *MAY* AND *MIGHT* FOR POSSIBILITY

Rewrite the sentences. Use **may** *or* **might**.

1. Maybe it will snow.

   It may snow. (OR: It might snow.)

2. Perhaps we'll come by taxi.

   _____

3. Perhaps he won't want to come.

   _____

4. Maybe they'll study.

_____

5. Perhaps the store will be closed.

_____

6. Maybe she won't finish the work by Friday.

_____

7. Maybe the dog will come home.

_____

8. Perhaps you won't like that kind of food.

_____

9. Maybe I won't leave before seven o'clock.

_____

10. Perhaps the cookies won't taste good.

_____

3 WILL FOR DEFINITE FUTURE VS. MAY FOR POSSIBILITY

Complete the sentences. Use **may** *or* **will**.

1. Tomorrow is my birthday. I _____will_____ be twenty-five.

2. I'm tall. My children _____may_____ be tall, too.

3. I don't know anything about that movie. It _____ not be good.

4. Are you taking a trip to the United States? You _____ need a passport. Everybody from Brazil needs one.

5. Don't worry. I _____ do it. I promise.

6. Ask about the price. It _____ be expensive.

7. The supermarket _____ sell flowers, but I'm not sure.

8. There's someone at the door. I _____ open it.

9. The sun _____ rise tomorrow.

10. The food _____ be ready. I'm going to look.

4 AFFIRMATIVE AND NEGATIVE STATEMENTS WITH *MAY* AND *MIGHT*

*Complete the sentences. Use **may (not)** or **might (not)** and the words in the box.*

bite	close	get lost	have an accident	~~pass~~
break	~~fall~~	get sick	live	win

1. Janet is worried about her little boy. He's climbing a tree.

   He ___may fall. (OR: might fall.)___

2. Jimmy has a test today, and he didn't study.

   He ___may not pass. (OR: might not pass.)___

3. Lynn is driving fast.

   She _____

4. Wrap those glasses carefully.

   They _____

5. Mark Muller is one of the top tennis players in the world, but he isn't playing well today.

   He _____

6. Don't lose these directions. It's difficult to find my house.

   You _____

7. The woman's injuries are very bad.

   She _____

8. Don't go near that animal.

   It _____

9. Don't go outside with wet hair. It's cold.

   You _____

10. That store never has many customers.

    It _____

DESIRES, INVITATIONS, REQUESTS: WOULD LIKE, WOULD YOU LIKE . . . ?, WOULD YOU PLEASE . . . ?

1 AFFIRMATIVE STATEMENTS AND QUESTIONS
WITH *WOULD LIKE*

Read each conversation. Then answer the question.

Conversation A

A: Can I help you?
B: Yes, I'd like two tickets to Pittsburgh.
A: Would you like one-way or round-trip?
B: Round-trip, please.
A: That's $38.90.
B: Here you are. What time is the next bus?
A: At 9:30.
B: Thank you.

1. Where does Conversation A take place?

_____

Conversation B

A: Sir, would you like chicken or fish?
B: Chicken, please.
A: And what would you like to drink?
B: Just some water, please.
A: And your wife?
B: She doesn't want anything. She doesn't like airplane food.

2. Where does Conversation B take place?

_____

Conversation C

A: Where would you like to sit?
B: These seats are fine. I don't want to sit too close to the screen.
A: Would you like some popcorn?
B: No, but I'd like something to drink. But hurry! The movie's going to start.

3. Where does Conversation C take place?

_____

2 AFFIRMATIVE STATEMENTS AND *YES / NO* QUESTIONS WITH *WOULD LIKE*

Rewrite the sentences. Use **would like**.

1. I want two airmail stamps.

   I would like two airmail stamps.

2. Do you want to have dinner with me?

   Would you like to have dinner with me?

3. Sheila wants to talk to you.

   _____

4. Do your parents want to come?

   _____

5. Sandy and Billy want some coffee.

   _____

6. Does Dan want to come with us?

   _____

7. My friend and I want a table for two.

   _____

8. Does the teacher want to come to the party?

   _____

9. I want to take a long trip.

   _____

10. We want you to have dinner with us.

    _____

❸ WOULD LIKE + OBJECT + INFINITIVE

Ari is planning a surprise birthday party for his roommate, Tony. He needs help from his friends. Look at his list. Write sentences. Use **would like**.

Surprise Birthday Party

Jerry—do some of the shopping

Conchita—bring the CDs

Irene and Amira—help with the cooking

Eric—bring his CD player

Harry, Mike, and Tom—move the furniture

Ellen—buy some ice cream

Victor—pick up the birthday cake

Carmen and Ted—keep Tony busy

Ratana—make the decorations

---

1. Ari would like Jerry to do some of the shopping.

2. _____

3. _____

4. _____

5. _____

6. _____

7. _____

8. _____

9. _____

④ STATEMENTS AND QUESTIONS WITH *WOULD LIKE*

Complete the conversation. Use the words in parentheses.

DAVE: Hi, Ellen. Come on in.

ELLEN: Hi, Dave. Thanks.

DAVE: _____Would you like_____ some coffee?
　　　　　　　　　　1. (you / like)

ELLEN: Yes. That sounds good. _____ some help?
　　　　　　　　　　　　　　　　　2. (you / like)

DAVE: No, it's ready. Here you are.

ELLEN: Thanks.

DAVE: _____ some cookies, too?
　　　　　　3. (you / like)

ELLEN: No, thanks, but I _____ some sugar for my coffee.
　　　　　　　　　　　　　　4. (like)

DAVE: Oh, sorry. I forgot. Here's the sugar.

ELLEN: Boy, it's cold outside.

DAVE: _____ you a sweater?
　　　　　　　5. (you / like / me / give)

ELLEN: No, I'm okay.

DAVE: So, _____ this evening?
　　　　　　6. (what / you / like / do)

ELLEN: I don't know. _____?
　　　　　　　　　　　　7. (Where / you / like / go)

DAVE: _____ to the movies?
　　　　8. (you / like / go)

ELLEN: What's playing?

DAVE: *Forever Love* is at the Rex. _____ that?
　　　　　　　　　　　　　　　　9. (you / like / see)

ELLEN: Okay. What time does it start?

DAVE: We can go at six, eight, or ten.

ELLEN: I don't care. _____?
　　　　　　　　　　10. (What time / you / like / go)

DAVE: Eight is fine, but I _____ something to eat
　　　　　　　　　　　　　　11. (like / get)

　　　　first.

ELLEN: Okay. _____?
　　　　　　12. (Where / you / like / eat)

DAVE: How about John's Pizzeria?

ELLEN: That sounds good.

5 *WOULD* AND *COULD* FOR POLITE REQUESTS

Write correct questions. Use **please** *with* **would you** *or* **could you.**

1. Ask a stranger on the bus to tell you the time.

   Would you please tell me the time? (OR: Could you please tell me the time?)

2. Ask a desk clerk at a hotel to give you the key to your room.

   _____

3. Ask your teacher to explain the meaning of the word *grateful*.

   _____

4. Ask a cashier to give you change for a dollar.

   _____

5. Ask a stranger to take a picture of you and your friends.

   _____

6. Ask a taxi driver to take you to the airport.

   _____

7. Ask a neighbor to help you with your suitcases.

   _____

8. Ask a sales clerk to show you the brown shoes in the window.

   _____

9. Ask the person in front of you at a basketball game to sit down.

   _____

UNIT 38

COMPARATIVE FORM OF ADJECTIVES

1 COMPARATIVE FORM OF ADJECTIVES

Put a check (✓) next to the statements that are true. (Look at your Student Book if you need help.)

_____ **1.** Carol is neater than Yoko is.

_____ **2.** Lulu is older than Pete is.

_____ **3.** Doug is younger than Carol is.

_____ **4.** Carol is more hardworking than Norma is.

_____ **5.** Yoko is more interested in her studies than Carol is.

_____ **6.** Lulu is busier than Pete is.

_____ **7.** Yoko is farther from home than Carol is.

2 COMPARATIVE FORM OF ADJECTIVES

Put the words in the box in the correct columns.

~~big~~	difficult	heavy	messy
~~careful~~	easy	high	noisy
~~comfortable~~	expensive	hot	old
crowded	fast	intelligent	pretty
dangerous	friendly	long	small

One Syllable	Two Syllables	Three or Four Syllables
big	careful	comfortable

3 COMPARATIVE FORM OF ADJECTIVES

Complete the sentences. Use the comparative form of the adjectives.

1. That car is old, but this car is ___older_____.

2. That book is good, but this book is _____.

3. The train station is far, but the airport is _____.

4. Tom is intelligent, but his brother is _____.

5. The service at that restaurant is bad, but the food is _____.

6. My sister's messy, but my brother is _____.

7. This chair is comfortable, but that chair is _____.

8. My husband is careful, but his father is _____.

9. This picture is pretty, but that picture is _____.

10. Chemistry is difficult, but physics is _____.

11. This exercise is easy, but the last exercise was _____.

4 COMPARATIVE FORM OF ADJECTIVES

Complete the sentences with the correct adjectives. Use the comparative form of the adjectives in parentheses and **than**.

1. San Francisco is _____smaller than_____ New York.
   (big / small)

2. The Nile River is _____ the Mississippi River.
   (long / short)

3. A Mercedes is _____ a Volkswagen.
   (cheap / expensive)

4. An ocean is _____ a lake.
   (big / small)

5. Mountains are _____ hills.
   (low / high)

6. Egypt is _____ Canada.
   (cold / hot)

7. Skiing is _____ golf.
   (safe / dangerous)

(continued on next page)

8. Cities are _____ villages.
   (crowded / empty)

9. Cars are _____ bicycles.
   (noisy / quiet)

10. A rock is _____ a leaf.
    (heavy / light)

11. Rabbits are _____ snails.
    (slow / fast)

12. Dogs are _____ wolves.
    (friendly / unfriendly)

⑤ COMPARATIVE FORM OF ADJECTIVES

Write questions. Use the comparative form of the adjectives. Then answer the questions.

1. Carol / neat / or / messy / Yoko

   _____Is Carol neater or messier than Yoko?_____   _____Carol is messier._____

2. this unit / easy / or / difficult / the last unit

   _____   _____

3. this watch / cheap / or / expensive / that watch

   _____   _____

4. you / young / or / old / your best friend

   _____   _____

5. you / tall / or / short / your teacher

   _____   _____

6. your hometown / big / or / small / Los Angeles

   _____   _____

7. today's weather / good / or / bad / yesterday's weather

   _____   _____

ADVERBS OF MANNER AND COMPARATIVE FORMS OF ADVERBS

 ADJECTIVES VS. ADVERBS

Write **adjective** *if the underlined word is an adjective. Write* **adverb** *if it is an adverb.*

1. Norma works <u>hard</u>. _____adverb_____

2. Carol's room is <u>dirty</u>. _____adjective_____

3. Pete drives <u>slowly</u>. _____

4. This exercise isn't <u>hard</u>. _____

5. Everyone's going to come <u>early</u>. _____

6. Carol did <u>badly</u> on the test. _____

7. Don't drive <u>fast</u>. _____

8. The food smells <u>good</u>. _____

9. That shirt is <u>ugly</u>. _____

10. I want to speak English <u>fluently</u>. _____

11. Carry these glasses <u>carefully</u>. _____

12. I was <u>tired</u> yesterday. _____

2 ADVERBS OF MANNER

Circle the ten adverbs in the box.

```
B  H  A  P  P  I  L  Y  F  A  X  M
A  E  A  S  I  L  Y  Q  A  X  D  O
D  A  N  G  E  R  O  U  S  L  Y  S
L  V  G  X  X  C  X  I  T  E  X  X
Y  I  R  P  A  T  I  E  N  T  L  Y
X  L  I  A  F  X  X  T  O  C  X  D
E  Y  L  S  W  E  L  L  B  N  O  R
X  X  Y  N  X  N  L  Y  I  K  X  E
```

3 ADVERBS OF MANNER

Complete the sentences. Use the adverbs in Exercise 2.

1. It's snowing _____heavily_____. We can't drive in this weather.

2. Please talk _____. The baby's sleeping.

3. Vinny drives _____. One day he's going to have an accident.

4. Lenore was an hour late for class. Her teacher looked at her _____.

5. The children played with their toys _____.

6. She plays the guitar very _____. Everyone loves to listen to her.

7. I never eat my father's food. He cooks _____.

8. I can't understand him. He speaks _____.

9. I waited _____, but the doctor never came.

10. Your directions were very good. I found the restaurant _____.

④ ADJECTIVES VS. ADVERBS

Complete the conversations. Use the adjectives in the box or their
adverb forms.

angry	easy	loud
beautiful	fast	~~quiet~~
careful	good	tired

1. **A:** Shh! Be _____quiet_____! The baby's sleeping.

   B: Okay. I'll open the door _____quietly_____.

2. **A:** The flowers are _____.

   B: They smell _____, too.

3. **A:** Is Gerry a _____ eater?

   B: Yes, she eats very _____. She always finishes dinner before me.

4. **A:** You look _____.

   B: I am _____. I'm going to bed.

5. **A:** Did Samara do _____ on the test?

   B: Yes. She got an A. She's a _____ student.

6. **A:** Does your daughter drive _____?

   B: Oh, yes. She's a very _____ driver. I never worry about her.

7. **A:** The music in that apartment is always _____.

   B: You're right. They play their music very _____.

8. **A:** Why did she leave the room so _____?

   B: I'm not sure. I think she was _____ with her boss.

9. **A:** That was an _____ test.

   B: I agree. I answered all the questions very _____.

5 COMPARATIVE FORMS OF ADVERBS

Complete the conversations. Use the comparative form of the adverb.

1. **A:** Did Ruben come early?

   B: Yes, but I came _____ *earlier* _____.

2. **A:** Does Alejandro work hard?

   B: Yes, but En Mi works _____.

3. **A:** Did your team play well?

   B: Yes, but the other team played _____.

4. **A:** Does Andrew type carefully?

   B: Yes, but Brian types _____.

5. **A:** Did the waiter yesterday serve you fast?

   B: Yes, but the waiter last week served us _____.

6. **A:** Does Adam write neatly?

   B: Yes, but his sister writes _____.

7. **A:** Does your husband dance badly?

   B: Yes, but I dance _____.

8. **A:** Does the mechanic on Elm Street fix cars quickly?

   B: Yes, but the mechanic on Diamond Street fixes them _____.

9. **A:** Did you learn to ride a bike easily?

   B: Yes, but my younger brother learned _____.

10. **A:** Can you jump high?

    B: Yes, but Charlie can jump _____.

11. **A:** Did the cashier speak to you rudely?

    B: Yes, but the manager spoke to me _____.

ADJECTIVE + ENOUGH / TOO / VERY; AS + ADJECTIVE / ADVERB + AS

 TOO AND **ENOUGH**

Match the questions and answers.

1. __b__ What's wrong with the soup?
2. ____ Do you want to go to that restaurant?
3. ____ Can you hear the music?
4. ____ Why are they playing baseball without you?
5. ____ Do you like boxing?
6. ____ Are you going to wear that dress?
7. ____ Do you drive?
8. ____ Are you happy with your grade on the test?

a. No, it's too violent.
b. It's too salty.
c. I'm not good enough.
d. No, it's too tight.
e. No, I'm not old enough
f. No, it's too crowded.
g. No, it isn't high enough.
h. No, the radio's not loud enough.

② **TOO + ADJECTIVE**

*Rewrite the sentences. Use **too**.*

1. The bathing suit isn't dry enough to wear.

   The bathing suit is too wet to wear.

2. The apartment isn't big enough for six people.

   _____

3. Shirley and Jack aren't fast enough to run in the race.

   _____

4. The car isn't cheap enough to buy.

   _____

(continued on next page)

185

5. The children aren't old enough to start school.

_____

6. The room isn't warm enough.

_____

③ ADJECTIVE + *NOT ENOUGH*

Rewrite the sentences. Use **not enough**.

1. It's too cold to sit outside.

   It isn't warm enough to sit outside. _____

2. The jacket is too small for me.

_____

3. The break was too short.

_____

4. It's too dark to take a picture.

_____

5. It's too noisy to talk.

_____

6. Buses are too slow.

_____

④ *TOO* AND *VERY*

Complete the sentences. Use **too** *or* **very**.

1. A: Do you like my new dress?

   B: Yes, it's _____ very _____ pretty.

2. A: Put these sweaters in the drawer.

   B: I can't. The drawer's _____ full.

3. A: Mommy, I want to swim in the baby pool.

   B: You're _____ big. You're not a baby.

4. A: What do you think of that hotel?

   B: The rooms are _____ nice, but it's expensive.

5. A: How's the weather in Montreal in January?

   B: It's _____ cold.

6. A: Can you read that sign?

   B: No, it's _____ far away.

7. A: Are you going to buy the stereo?

   B: I think so. The price is _____ good.

8. A: The floor's _____ dirty.

   B: I'll wash it.

9. A: Put this bag in your pocket.

   B: I can't. It's _____ big.

5 TOO OR *ENOUGH* + INFINITIVE

Combine the sentences. Use **too** *or* **enough** *and an infinitive.*

1. I can't watch the movie. It's too sad.

   The movie is too sad to watch.

2. I can't drink this coffee. It's too strong.

   _____

3. Pete did not understand the instructions. They were too difficult.

   _____

4. We can't eat the fruit. It's not ripe enough.

   _____

5. We can't wait. The line's too long.

   _____

6. She didn't wash the sweater by hand. It was too dirty.

   _____

(continued on next page)

7. You can't marry him. He's not rich enough.

_____

8. You can eat the eggs. They're cooked enough.

_____

6 TOO, ENOUGH, AND NOT ENOUGH

Complete the conversations. Use **too**, **enough**, *or* **not enough** *and the adjective in parentheses.*

1. A: Why did you take the pants back to the store?

    B: They were _____ *too long* _____. I exchanged them for a shorter pair.
                                  (long)

2. A: Do you want me to wash the car again?

    B: Yes. It's _____ *not clean enough* _____.
                         (clean)

3. A: Let's go into that big old house. I want to see what's in there.

    B: No, I'm _____. There may be ghosts.
                       (frightened)

4. A: Are the shoes comfortable?

    B: No, they're _____. I need a size 8, and they're a size 7.
                          (big)

5. A: Why didn't you get the tickets?

    B: It was _____. There weren't any left.
                      (late)

6. A: Is the soup _____?
                        (hot)
    B: Yeah. Thanks for heating it up.

7. A: How are the pants?

    B: They're _____. I think I need a larger size.
                    (tight)

8. A: Why do I need to rewrite this composition?

    B: Because it's _____. It's only 150 words, and I told you to
                      (short)
    write at least 250 words.

9. A: Can I borrow your bike?

    B: No, there's something wrong with the brakes. It's _____ to ride.
                                           (safe)

10. A: Dad, can we go in the water now?

   B: I don't know. It was cold before. Put your toe in the water and see if it's

   _____ now.
   (warm)

11. A: Why aren't the plants in the living room growing?

   B: Probably because it's _____. They need more light.
   (sunny)

7 AS + ADJECTIVE + AS, *THE SAME* (+ NOUN) *AS, DIFFERENT FROM*

Put a check (✓) next to the sentences that are true.

_____ **1.** Canada is the same size as the United States.

_____ **2.** Lions are not as big as elephants.

_____ **3.** 32° F is the same temperature as 0° C.

_____ **4.** The Statue of Liberty in New York is not as old as the Pyramids in Egypt.

_____ **5.** Alaska is as cold as Antarctica.

_____ **6.** A whale is different from a fish.

_____ **7.** An orange is the same color as a carrot.

_____ **8.** Silver is as valuable as gold.

8 THAN VS. AS

Complete the sentences. Use **as** *or* **than.**

1. Russia is bigger _____*than*_____ the United States.

2. Is your classroom the same size _____*as*_____ the other classrooms?

3. South America is not as big _____ Asia.

4. English is more difficult _____ my native language.

5. The president of the United States is not the same age _____ the leader of my country.

6. I'm more tired today _____ I was yesterday.

7. Are doctors as rich _____ lawyers?

8. Are you as thin _____ your best friend?

(continued on next page)

9. Thelma's the same height _____ her brother.

10. Are animals more intelligent _____ human beings?

11. This book is better _____ that one.

12. Some people are friendlier _____ others.

❾ AS + ADJECTIVE + AS VS. MORE + ADJECTIVE + THAN

Write sentences. Use the adjective in parentheses and **as . . . as,**
not as . . . as, *or* **more . . . than.** *(Remember:* = *means* **equals,**
< *means* **less than;** > *means* **more than.***)*

1. a Fiat < a Mercedes (expensive)

   A Fiat isn't as expensive as a Mercedes.

2. the book > the film (interesting)

   The book is more interesting than the film.

3. my apartment = your apartment (big)

   My apartment is as big as your apartment.

4. trains < airplanes (fast)

5. January = February (cold)

6. the chair = the sofa (comfortable)

7. the governor of Oregon < the president of the United States (famous)

8. the bank < the post office (far)

9. limes = lemons (sour)

10. jazz > rock music (relaxing)

11. chocolate ice cream < vanilla ice cream (good)

_____

12. some people > other people (violent)

_____

13. college < high school (easy)

_____

14. these boxes = those boxes (heavy)

_____

🔟 THE SAME + NOUN + AS

Write questions. Use **the same . . . as** *and a noun in the box.*

> age   distance   ~~color~~   height   length   price   size   weight

1. ___Is your sister's hair the same color as your hair?_____

No. My sister's hair is brown. My hair's black.

2. _____

No. I'm 1.69 meters tall. My brother's 1.78 meters tall.

3. _____

No. My mother's fifty-nine years old. My father's sixty-two.

4. _____

No. The dining room's smaller than the living room.

5. _____

Yes. The apples and the oranges are both sixty cents a pound.

6. _____

No. I'm thinner than my brother.

7. _____

No. *War and Peace* is much longer than *Crime and Punishment*.

8. _____

No. The subway station is farther than the bus stop.

11 *THE SAME AS* AND *DIFFERENT FROM*

Write sentences. Use **the same as** *or* **different from**.

1. a wife and a housewife

   A wife is different from a housewife.

2. the U.S.A. and the United States

   The U.S.A. is the same as the United States.

3. a bike and a bicycle

4. a TV and a television

5. North America and the United States

6. 10,362 and 10.362

7. 3×16 and 16×3

8. $16 \div 3$ and $3 \div 16$

9. $1 and £1

10. a snack bar and a restaurant

11. 12:00 P.M. and noon

12. a plane and an airplane

THE PAST PROGRESSIVE

① AFFIRMATIVE AND NEGATIVE STATEMENTS WITH THE PAST PROGRESSIVE

Put a check (✓) next to the sentences that are true.

_____ **1.** I was sleeping at six o'clock yesterday morning.

_____ **2.** While I was having dinner last night, the telephone rang.

_____ **3.** A year ago I was not studying English.

_____ **4.** Last week I saw a friend when I was walking down the street.

_____ **5.** My classmates and I were not taking a test at this time last week.

_____ **6.** While I was getting dressed yesterday, birds were singing outside my window.

_____ **7.** My family and I were watching TV at 9:30 last night.

_____ **8.** While I was doing my homework yesterday, I made some mistakes.

② AFFIRMATIVE STATEMENTS WITH THE PAST PROGRESSIVE

What were these people doing? Make guesses and write sentences. Use the words in the box and the past progressive.

buy some groceries	go to school	talk on the phone	~~wait for the bus~~
cook dinner	study	type	wait for a table
get gas	take a shower		

1. I saw Lulu and Bertha at the bus stop.

   They were waiting for the bus.

2. I called Lulu yesterday, but her line was busy.

3. I saw Uncle Bob and Aunt Valerie at the Hillside Restaurant.

193

(continued on next page)

4. I saw Carol and Yoko at the library last night.

_____

5. I saw Pete's new secretary in the office.

_____

6. I saw Pete at the supermarket.

_____

7. When I called Elenore, she was in the bathroom.

_____

8. When I arrived at Norma's apartment, she was in the kitchen.

_____

9. When I went to the gas station, Milt was there.

_____

10. I saw Doug on 82nd Street.

_____

3 AFFIRMATIVE AND NEGATIVE STATEMENTS WITH THE PAST PROGRESSIVE

Write affirmative or negative sentences about the picture on page 47.
Use the past progressive.

1. When I saw Doug at the fruit store, he _____was standing_____ in line.
(stand)

2. When I saw Doug at the fruit store, he _____wasn't eating_____ an apple.
(eat)

3. When I saw Doug at the fruit store, he _____.
(read)

4. When I saw Doug at the fruit store, three other people _____
in line.
(wait)

5. When I saw Doug at the fruit store, the other people _____
in front of him.
(stand)

6. When I saw Doug at the fruit store, he _____ pants.
(wear)

7. When I saw Doug at the fruit store, he _____ his
history book.
(hold)

8. When I saw Doug at the fruit store, he (buy) _____ bananas.
   (buy)

9. When I saw Doug at the fruit store, the other customers _____.
   (leave)

4 **THE SIMPLE PAST AND THE PAST PROGRESSIVE**

Write sentences. Use the past progressive and the simple past in each sentence.

1. When / the teacher / ask / me a question / I / read

   When the teacher asked me a question, I was reading.

2. While / my father / talk / to me / someone / ring / the doorbell

   _____

3. The boys / play / basketball / when / the fight / start

   _____

4. I / swim / when / I / get / a pain in my leg

   _____

5. When / we / see / the accident / we / drive / down Market Street

   _____

6. The doctor / examine / Mrs. May / when / she / scream

   _____

7. While / I / wash / my hair / I / get / some soap in my eyes

   _____

8. Alan / shave / when / he / cut / himself

   _____

9. The train / come / while / we / get / our tickets

   _____

5 **YES / NO QUESTIONS WITH THE PAST PROGRESSIVE**

Write questions. Use the past progressive.

1. **A:** Simon and Barbara have breakfast between 7:00 and 7:30 every morning.

   B: ___Were they having breakfast___ yesterday morning at 7:15?

   A: I think so.

2. **A:** Simon meets with his salespeople every morning between 9:00 and 9:30.

   B: _____ at 9:20 yesterday morning?

   A: Probably.

3. **A:** Barbara teaches every day between one o'clock and four o'clock.

   B: _____ yesterday at three o'clock?

   A: Of course.

4. **A:** Simon swims every Monday and Wednesday between noon and 12:45.

   B: _____ last Wednesday at 12:30?

   A: Probably.

5. **A:** Barbara practices the piano every morning between 9:00 and 10:00.

   B: _____ at 9:30 yesterday morning?

   A: Almost definitely.

6. **A:** Simon listens to a business report on the radio every afternoon between 4:30 and 5:00.

   B: _____ at 4:45 yesterday afternoon?

   A: I guess so.

7. **A:** Simon and Barbara have dinner between six o'clock and seven o'clock.

   B: _____ at 6:30 yesterday?

   A: Yes.

8. A: Simon and Barbara watch the news every evening between 7:00 and 7:30.

   B: _____ yesterday evening at 7:15?

   A: I think so.

9. A: Barbara takes a bath every evening between 9:00 and 9:30.

   B: _____ at 9:15 yesterday evening?

   A: Probably.

6 THE SIMPLE PAST VS. THE PAST PROGRESSIVE

Answer the questions. Use the simple past or the past progressive of the verbs in parentheses.

1a. A: What were you doing when it started to rain?

   B: We _____ were having _____ a picnic.
                    (have)

1b. A: What did you do when it started to rain?

   B: We _____ to the car.
                    (hurry)

2a. A: What were you doing when the phone rang?

   B: I _____ TV.
              (watch)

2b. A: What did you do when the phone rang?

   B: I _____ it.
              (answer)

3a. A: What were the children doing when the fire started?

   B: They _____.
                   (sleep)

3b. A: What did the children do when the fire started?

   B: They _____ out of the house.
                   (run)

4a. A: What were you doing when the teacher came in?

   B: We _____ around.
                   (stand)

4b. A: What did you do when the teacher came in?

   B: We _____ down.
              (sit)

(continued on next page)

5a. A: What was Susan doing when she fell?

B: She _____ a tree.
(climb)

5b. A: What did Susan do when she fell?

B: She _____ her mother.
(call)

6a. A: What was your father doing when he burned his hand?

B: He _____.
(iron)

6b. A: What did your father do when he burned his hand?

B: He _____ some ice on the burn.
(put)

⑦ WH- QUESTIONS WITH THE PAST PROGRESSIVE

Write questions. Use **who, what, when, where, why,** *or* **how fast** *and the verbs in the box.*

do	drive	go	ride	~~stand~~	wait

1. A: ___Where were you standing___ when the accident happened?

B: I was standing on the corner of Buick and 3rd Street.

2. A: _____?

B: I was waiting.

3. A: _____?

B: I was waiting for the bus.

4. A: _____?

B: I was going to the gym.

5. A: _____?

B: Because I always go to the gym on Mondays.

6. A: _____ the red car?

   B: A teenager was driving it.

7. A: _____?

B: He was going at least 65 miles per hour.

8. A: _____?

B: I don't know. Maybe he was driving so fast because the passenger was ill.

9. A: _____ in the car with him?

   B: An older woman. Maybe it was his mother.

UNIT 42

SHOULD, SHOULDN'T, OUGHT TO, HAD BETTER, AND HAD BETTER NOT

1 AFFIRMATIVE AND NEGATIVE STATEMENTS WITH SHOULD

Complete the sentences. Use **should** *or* **shouldn't**.

1. Children ___shouldn't___ play with matches.

2. Children _____ watch television all day long.

3. Children _____ listen to their parents.

4. Children _____ eat a lot of candy.

5. Children _____ play in the street.

6. Teenagers _____ pay attention in school.

7. Teenagers _____ keep their bedrooms neat.

8. Teenagers _____ stay out all night with their friends.

9. Adults _____ exercise at least twice a week.

10. Adults _____ drink ten cups of coffee a day.

2 AFFIRMATIVE STATEMENTS WITH OUGHT TO

Rewrite the sentences. Use **ought to**.

1. You should go to the dentist twice a year.

   You ought to go to the dentist twice a year.

2. I should visit my grandparents more often.

   _____

3. All passengers should arrive at the airport an hour before their flights.

   _____

4. Carol should study harder.

_____

5. We should take something to the party.

_____

③ AFFIRMATIVE STATEMENTS WITH *SHOULD*

Rewrite the sentences. Use **should**.

1. Carol ought to clean her room more often.

_____ Carol should clean her room more often. _____

2. You ought to cook the meat a little longer.

_____

3. Lulu ought to be nicer to Elenore.

_____

4. I ought to learn how to type.

_____

5. Pete and Elenore ought to move into a smaller apartment.

_____

④ AFFIRMATIVE AND NEGATIVE STATEMENTS WITH *SHOULD*

Complete the sentences. Use **should** *or* **shouldn't** *and the words in the box.*

~~see a doctor~~	leave early	study more	wash it
go to the dentist	look for another one	touch it	watch it
leave a tip	smoke		

1. Dave is sick. He _____ should see a doctor. _____

2. I don't like my job. I _____

3. John often has a bad cough. He _____

(continued on next page)

4. Myra has a toothache. She _____

5. The car is dirty. We _____

6. The waiter is terrible. We _____

7. Doug and Jason aren't doing well in math. They _____

8. There's going to be a lot of traffic. We _____

9. That movie is very violent. The children _____

10. That dog may bite. You _____

5 WH- QUESTIONS WITH *SHOULD*

Complete the conversation. Write questions with **should***. Use* **who,**
what, when, where, why, *or* **how many** *and the verbs in parentheses.*

A: Let's have a party.

B: Okay. _____ When should we have _____ it?
    1. (have)

A: Let's have it on March 23rd.

B: _____ it then?
        2. (have)

A: Because it's Lucy's birthday.

B: Oh, that's right. _____?
                    3. (invite)

A: Probably around twenty-five people.

B: _____?
        4. (invite)

A: Let's see . . . the neighbors, Lucy's family, the people from the office.

B: _____?
        5. (buy)

A: Well, we'll need drinks, potato chips, and things like that.

B: _____?
        6. (cook)

A: I'll make some lasagna.

B: That sounds good. I'll make some salad. _____ a
    birthday cake?   **7. (get)**

A: I like the Savoy Bakery's cakes.

B: Okay. Let's order one from there.

A: You know, we don't have enough dishes and glasses for twenty-five people.

_____?
8. (do)

B: That's no problem. We can get paper plates and cups at the supermarket.

A: You're right. That's a good idea. _____ out the invitations?
9. (send)

B: I'll write them this weekend.

❻ AFFIRMATIVE AND NEGATIVE STATEMENTS WITH *HAD BETTER*

Match the situations with the advice.

__c__ **1.** We'd better take a taxi.

_____ **2.** We'd better ask for directions.

_____ **3.** We'd better not stay up late.

_____ **4.** We'd better make sure everything is locked.

_____ **5.** We'd better look at a map.

_____ **6.** We'd better not wait for the bus.

_____ **7.** We'd better not stay in the sun anymore.

_____ **8.** We'd better get a good night's sleep.

_____ **9.** We'd better throw away the food in the refrigerator.

_____ **10.** We'd better put some cream on our arms and legs.

a. We're lost.

b. We're getting red.

c. We're going to be late.

d. We'll be away for three weeks.

e. We have an exam tomorrow.

7 AFFIRMATIVE AND NEGATIVE STATEMENTS WITH *HAD BETTER*

Don and Amy are planning a dinner party. Complete the conversation.
Use **had better** *or* **had better not** *and the words in the box.*

ask Costas to bring her	invite him	rent a video
borrow some from the neighbors	let the dog in the house	serve shrimp
get a couple of bottles	~~make roast beef~~	sit together at the table

DON: What kind of food should we make? How about roast beef?

AMY: Alan can't eat beef.

DON: Well, then we _____ had better not make roast beef _____. How about shrimp?
                                                    1.

AMY: Joan doesn't like fish or seafood.

DON: Then we _____. How about chicken?
                              2.

AMY: Good idea. Do we have enough drinks?

DON: Ed drinks only Diet Coke. We _____. Is Chris
                                                        3.

coming? She's allergic to animals. We _____.
                                                              4.

AMY: How is Sandy getting here? She doesn't drive and lives far from here.

DON: We _____.
                        5.

AMY: What do you think of the seating plan?

DON: Marsha and Sophia _____. They don't like each
                                              6.

other.

AMY: I just remembered Tonya has a new boyfriend. We

_____. And Ted and Marsha are bringing their
              7.

children.

DON: They will probably get bored. We _____.
                                                        8.

AMY: How many guests are coming? We won't have enough chairs.

DON: We _____.
                        9.

HAVE TO, DON'T HAVE TO, MUST, MUSTN'T

❶ PRESENT AND PAST AFFIRMATIVE AND NEGATIVE STATEMENTS WITH *HAVE TO*

Put a check (✓) next to the sentences that are true.

_____ **1.** People in my country have to pay taxes.

_____ **2.** People in my country don't have to vote.

_____ **3.** Drivers in my country have to have driver's licenses.

_____ **4.** Students in my country don't have to wear uniforms in high school.

_____ **5.** Young people in my country don't have to do military service.

_____ **6.** Women in my country had to obey their husbands fifty years ago.

_____ **7.** Children in my country did not have to go to school fifty years ago.

_____ **8.** Children in my country had to go to work at a young age fifty years ago.

❷ AFFIRMATIVE AND NEGATIVE STATEMENTS WITH *HAVE TO*

Complete the sentences. Use **have to** *and* **don't have to** *in each sentence.*

1. Students _don't have to_ stay in school twelve hours a day, but they

have to study.

2. Teachers _____ correct papers, but they _____

wear uniforms.

3. Police officers _____ speak a foreign language, but they

_____ wear uniforms.

4. Doctors _____ study for many years, but they

_____ know how to type.

205

(continued on next page)

5. Secretaries _____ work at night, but they _____ know how to type.

6. Firefighters _____ work at night, but they _____ study for many years.

7. Fashion models _____ work seven days a week, but they _____ worry about their appearance.

8. Farmers _____ get up early in the morning, but they _____ worry about their appearance.

9. Basketball players _____ practice regularly, but they _____ play a game every day.

10. Accountants _____ be good writers, but they _____ be good with numbers.

---

3 **AFFIRMATIVE AND NEGATIVE STATEMENTS WITH *HAVE TO***

Complete the conversations. Use **have to**, **has to**, **don't have to**, *or* **doesn't have to**.

1. **A:** Is Dan getting up early this morning?

   B: No, he *doesn't have to get up early this morning*. There's no school.

2. **A:** Is Sheila leaving early today?

   B: Yes, she _____. She has an appointment with her dentist.

3. **A:** Are you going food shopping today?

   B: Yes, I _____. There's no food in the house.

4. **A:** Are you and your wife coming by taxi?

   B: Yes, we _____. Our car isn't working.

5. **A:** Is Barbara working late today?

   B: No, she _____. Her boss is on vacation.

6. **A:** Are the children cleaning up their room?

   B: No, they _____. I cleaned it up yesterday.

7. **A:** Is Mary taking some medicine?

   B: Yes, she _____. She has a stomach problem.

8. **A:** Are you paying for the tickets?

   B: No, we _____. They're free.

9. **A:** Is José wearing a suit and tie this morning?

   B: Yes, he _____. He has an important business

   meeting.

10. **A:** Does Bonnie do housework?

    B: No, she _____. She has a maid.

---

4 PRESENT AND PAST AFFIRMATIVE AND NEGATIVE STATEMENTS WITH *HAVE TO*

Rewrite the sentences. Use **have to**, **has to**, **don't have to**, **doesn't have to**, **had to**, *or* **didn't have to**.

1. It's necessary for me to finish this exercise.

   I _have to finish this exercise._

2. It isn't necessary for me to do the last exercise again.

   I _____

3. It wasn't necessary for Doug to go to school yesterday.

   Doug _____

4. It was necessary for Carol to clean her room yesterday.

   Carol _____

5. It isn't necessary for Yoko to write her parents every week.

   Yoko _____

6. It wasn't necessary for Pete and Elenore to go shopping last week.

   Pete and Elenore _____

7. It's necessary for my classmates and me to take tests.

   My classmates and I _____

8. It isn't necessary for Pete and Elenore to buy a new car.

   Pete and Elenore _____

(continued on next page)

9. It's necessary for Lulu to see her doctor today.

Lulu _____

10. It's necessary for me to check my answers to this exercise.

I _____

5 AFFIRMATIVE AND NEGATIVE STATEMENTS WITH *MUST*

What does each sign mean? Write sentences. Use **must** *or* **mustn't** *and the words in the box.*

drive faster than 55 mph	make a U-turn	stop
~~enter~~	park in this area	turn left
go more slowly	pass	turn right

1.

DO NOT ENTER

2.

STOP

3.

4.

5.

SPEED LIMIT 55

6.

NO PARKING ANY TIME

7.

8.

9.

MEN AT WORK

1. _You mustn't enter._____

2. _____

3. _____

4. _____

5. _____

6. _____

7. _____

8. _____

9. _____

6 AFFIRMATIVE AND NEGATIVE STATEMENTS WITH *HAD TO*

Mr. and Mrs. Chung were on vacation last week. Write sentences. Use
had to *or* **didn't have to**.

do anything special	look for a hotel
find someone to take care of their dog	make the bed every morning
get to the airport on time	pack and unpack suitcases
get up early every morning	pay their hotel bill
go to work	wash dishes

1.   They didn't have to do anything special. _____

2.   _____

3.   _____

4.   _____

5.   _____

6.   _____

7.   _____

8.   _____

9.   _____

10. _____

7 PAST AND PRESENT *YES / NO* QUESTIONS AND SHORT ANSWERS WITH *HAVE TO*

*Write questions. Use **have to**. Then answer the questions. Use short answers.*

1. have / English / in class / you / to / do / speak

   Do you have to speak English in class?

   Yes, we do. (OR: No, we don't.)

2. get up / to / your / have / does / in the morning / at 6:00 / mother

   _____

   _____

3. you / to / last night / cook / did / have

   _____

   _____

4. best friend / do / does / to / have / your / this exercise

   _____

   _____

5. to / you / on time / in / have / English class / do / be

   _____

   _____

6. friends / learn / to / do / English / your / have

   _____

   _____

7. shave / father / have / your / did / to / yesterday

   _____

   _____

8. your / to work / to / best friend / yesterday / did / have / go

_____

_____

9. a / to / test / you / have / did / last week / take

_____

_____

8 PAST AND PRESENT _WH-_ QUESTIONS WITH _HAVE TO_

Write questions. Use **have to**.

1. I have to buy some food.

What _do you have to buy?_ _____

2. She has to get a book from the library.

Why _____

3. He has to go.

Where _____

4. The teacher had to talk to someone.

Who _____

5. We had to stay there a long time.

How long _____

6. The students have to stay after class.

Why _____

7. I have to use eggs.

How many eggs _____

8. The high school students had to send their college applications.

When _____

9. I have to get up early.

What time _____

10. He had to borrow some money.

How much money _____

UNIT

44 SUPERLATIVE FORM OF ADJECTIVES AND ADVERBS

1 THE SUPERLATIVE FORM OF ADJECTIVES AND ADVERBS

Answer the questions about the Winston family. Write **Carol**, **Doug**, *or* **Norma**. *(Look at your Student Book if you need help.)*

1. Who's the oldest? _____Norma_____

2. Who's the youngest? _____

3. Who's the neatest? _____

4. Who lives the farthest from home? _____

5. Who's the most serious of the three? _____

6. Who has the busiest social life? _____

2 THE SUPERLATIVE FORM OF ADJECTIVES

Complete the sentences. Use the superlative form of the adjective.

1. The kitchen is always hot. It's _____the hottest_____ room in the house.

2. Roger's a bad student. He's _____ student in the class.

3. Chemistry is hard. For me, it's _____ subject in school.

4. Roses are beautiful. In fact, many people think that roses are _____ flowers.

5. Noon is a busy time at the bank. In fact, it's _____ time.

212

6. "Married Young" is a funny program. It's _____ program on TV.

7. Scully's is a good restaurant. In fact, it's _____ restaurant in town.

8. I think monkeys are ugly. In my opinion, they're _____ animals in the zoo.

9. Midnight is a popular nightclub. It's _____ nightclub in town.

10. Dixon's has low prices. It has _____ prices in the neighborhood.

11. Pamela's a fast swimmer. She's _____ swimmer on the team.

12. Jake is charming. He's _____ of all my friends.

❸ THE COMPARATIVE AND SUPERLATIVE FORM OF ADJECTIVES

Write two sentences. Use the superlative form of the adjective in parentheses for one sentence. Use the comparative form for the other.

1. a train / a plane / a bus (fast)

   a. ___A plane is the fastest of the three.___

   b. ___A train is faster than a bus.___

2. a teenager / a child / a baby (old)

   a. _____

   b. _____

3. a Ford / a Rolls Royce / a BMW (expensive)

   a. _____

   b. _____

4. Nigeria / Spain / Sweden (hot)

   a. _____

   b. _____

(continued on next page)

5. a street / a path / a highway (wide)

    a. _____

    b. _____

6. a city / a village / a town (big)

    a. _____

    b. _____

7. an elephant / a gorilla / a fox (heavy)

    a. _____

    b. _____

8. an hour / a second / a minute (long)

    a. _____

    b. _____

9. boxing / golf / soccer (dangerous)

    a. _____

    b. _____

10. a banana / a carrot / chocolate (fattening)

    a. _____

    b. _____

4 THE SUPERLATIVE FORM OF ADVERBS

Write sentences. Use the superlative form of the adverbs in parentheses.

1. Andy came at 6:00. Mike came at 6:20. Jean came at 6:40.

    a. (late) _Jean came the latest._____

    b. (early) _____

2. The red car is going fifty miles per hour. The blue car is going sixty-five miles per hour. The white car's going seventy-three miles per hour.

    a. (slowly) _____

    b. (fast) _____

3. Shirley drives well and never has car accidents. Maurice usually drives well, but he had an accident last year. Fran drives badly. She had two accidents last year and one accident this year.

   a. (dangerously) _____

   b. (carefully) _____

4. Gary works two miles from his home. Viv works fifteen miles from her home. Harris works thirty miles from his home.

   a. (close) _____

   b. (far) _____

5. Milton speaks a few words of Spanish. Linda can speak Spanish, but she often makes mistakes. Carolyn speaks Spanish and never makes mistakes.

   a. (well) _____

   b. (badly) _____

6. Sam types fifty words a minute, but he always makes at least six mistakes. Joan types sixty words a minute, but she doesn't usually make any mistakes. Renée types seventy-five words a minute, but she often makes two or three mistakes.

   a. (quickly) _____

   b. (accurately) _____

PUTTING IT ALL TOGETHER

REVIEW OF VERB TENSES AND MODALS

1 VERB TENSE REVIEW

Find the thirteen verb tense mistakes in the postcard. Then correct them.

> *May 22nd*
>
> *Dear Mom and Dad,*
>
>   *Greetings from Venice. Dan and I* *~~am~~ fine. We have a wonderful time on our*
>
> *honeymoon. The weather isn't great, but Venice be such a romantic place. It have*
>
> *so many beautiful places.*
>
>   *Yesterday we walk all around the city. We visit several churches. They was so*
>
> *wonderful, and we see so many gorgeous paintings.*
>
>   *Today it rained all morning, so we didn't went far from our hotel. This afternoon*
>
> *we have lunch at a very good restaurant across from the hotel. We both eat special*
>
> *Venetian dishes and enjoyed them very much.*
>
>   *It is five o'clock now, and Dan rests. Tonight after dinner we take a gondola ride.*
>
> *I can't wait!*
>
>   *Love,*
>
>   *Carol*

2 VERB TENSE REVIEW AND *WH-* QUESTIONS

Read Carol's diary. Then write questions. Use **who, what, when, where, what time, how long,** *or* **why.**

> ### May 20th
>
> Venice is such a wonderful place. We arrived at eleven o'clock this morning, and I already love it. I still can't believe it, but we took a boat from the airport to our hotel on the Grand Canal. Tonight we're going to take a gondola ride.

1.   When did they arrive in Venice?

At eleven o'clock on May 20th.

2. _____

It's on the Grand Canal.

3. _____

They're going to take a gondola ride.

> ### May 21st
>
> Well, it rained all night last night, so we stayed in our hotel. I really wanted to go on the gondola ride, but it was impossible in the rain.
>
> Today we're going on a walking tour of the city. The tour will start at 9:00. (It's 7:30 now, and Dan is sleeping.) The tour guide is a professor of art history at the university here. I think it will be interesting.
>
> In the evening we're going to have dinner at a restaurant near Piazza San Marco with two people from Canada. We met them yesterday on the boat ride from the airport. Their names are Paul and Myra, and they're going to stay in Venice for two weeks.

(continued on next page)

4. _____

Because it rained all night.

5. _____

On a walking tour of the city.

6. _____

At 9:00.

7. _____

He's sleeping.

8. _____

A professor of art history.

9. _____

At a restaurant near Piazza San Marco.

10. _____

With two people from Canada.

11. _____

Yesterday.

12. _____

Paul and Myra.

13. _____

For two weeks.

> *May 22nd*
>
> *Dinner was great. Paul is a little strange, but I like Myra a lot. Paul*
> *and Dan ate too much. Dan was sick all night and didn't fall asleep*
> *until five in the morning. It's already 8:30, and he's still sleeping.*
> *Dan loves to sleep. (I didn't know that before the wedding. It's okay.*
> *I love him anyway!)*

14. _____

Myra.

15. _____

He ate too much.

16. _____

He loves to sleep.

---

3 **REVIEW OF MODALS**

How will Carol and Dan's life change after marriage? Complete the sentences. Circle the best answers and write them on the lines.

1. Carol and Dan _____*have to*_____ find a place to live.

    a. may

    (b.) have to

2. Dan _____ go out with other women.

    a. mustn't

    b. doesn't have to

3. Carol and Dan _____ buy a house.

    a. may

    b. must

4. Carol and Dan _____ have a lot of children.

    a. might

    b. have to

5. Carol _____ fight a lot with Dan.

    a. can't

    b. shouldn't

6. Carol and Dan _____ be honest with each other.

    a. can

    b. should

(continued on next page)

7. Carol and Dan _____ earn money.

   a. may

   b. have to

8. Carol's parents _____ say bad things about Dan.

   a. don't have to

   b. shouldn't

9. Carol and Dan _____ help each other with problems.

   a. ought to

   b. mustn't

10. Carol and Dan _____ listen to Carol's parents.

    a. can't

    b. don't have to

11. Carol _____ be rude to Dan's family.

    a. mustn't

    b. doesn't have to

REVIEW OF VERB TENSES AND COMPARISONS

1 COMPARATIVE FORM OF ADJECTIVES AND ADVERBS

Yoko had Teacher A this year and Teacher B last year. She liked Teacher A more. Here are the reasons. Compare the two teachers. Write sentences.

Teacher A	**Teacher B**
1. Teacher A is very patient.	Teacher B isn't very patient.
2. Teacher A is organized.	Teacher B isn't organized.
3. Teacher A is nice.	Teacher B isn't very nice.
4. Teacher A teaches well.	Teacher B doesn't teach well.
5. Teacher A speaks clearly.	Teacher B doesn't speak clearly.
6. Teacher A is friendly.	Teacher B isn't very friendly.
7. Teacher A gives back homework quickly.	Teacher B doesn't give back homework quickly.
8. Teacher A explains things slowly.	Teacher B doesn't explain things slowly.
9. The atmosphere in Teacher A's class is relaxed.	The atmosphere in Teacher B's class isn't relaxed.
10. The homework in Teacher A's class is easy.	The homework in Teacher B's class is difficult.
11. The books in Teacher A's class are interesting.	The books in Teacher B's class aren't very interesting.
12. Unfortunately, the tests in Teacher A's class are hard.	The tests in Teacher B's class aren't hard.

1. _Teacher A is more patient than Teacher B._____

2. _____

3. _____

4. _____

5. _____

6. _____

7. _____

8. _____

9. _____

10. _____

11. _____

12. _____

2 SENTENCES WITH *NOT AS . . . AS*

Rewrite the sentences in Exercise 4. Use **not as . . . as**.

1. Teacher B isn't as patient as Teacher A.

2. _____

3. _____

4. _____

5. _____

6. _____

7. _____

8. _____

9. _____

10. _____

11. _____

12. _____

REVIEW OF VERB TENSES, NOUNS, AND QUANTIFIERS

1 QUANTIFIERS AND COUNT AND NON-COUNT NOUNS

Find the ten differences between the pictures. Write sentences. Use **a few**, **a little**, *or* **a lot of**.

1. There are a few dishes in the first picture, but there are a lot of dishes in the second picture.

2. _____

_____

3. _____

_____

(continued on next page)

4. _____

_____

5. _____

_____

6. _____

_____

7. _____

_____

8. _____

_____

9. _____

_____

10. _____

_____

❷ YES / NO QUESTIONS WITH *MANY* AND *MUCH*

*Write questions about the first picture on page 223. Use **many** or **much**
and the words in the box. Then answer the questions.*

dishes	chairs	flowers	glasses
bread	cheese	fruit	orange juice
butter	chocolate	gifts	potato chips

1. _Are there many dishes?_____

_No, there aren't._____

2. _____

_____

3. _____

_____

4. _____

_____

5. _____

_____

6. _____

_____

7. _____

_____

8. _____

_____

9. _____

_____

10. _____

_____

11. _____

_____

12. _____

_____

ANSWER KEY

Where the full form is given, the contraction is also acceptable. Where the contracted form is given, the full form is also acceptable, unless the exercise is about contractions.

PART | THE VERB *BE*: PRESENT AND PAST

UNIT 1 THE PRESENT AFFIRMATIVE OF *BE*

1

2. We are
3. She is
4. He is
5. They are
6. I am
7. It is
8. They are
9. She is
10. You are

2

2. We
3. She
4. It
5. He
6. It
7. They
8. We
9. They
10. He
11. He
12. It

3

Sentences with: I am / My best friend is / My mother is / My father is / My teacher is / My parents are / My classmates are

4

2. We are here. That is wonderful.
3. Your food is on the table. Good! I am hungry.
4. Charlie is in love with Linda. But she is married.
5. I am sorry about the window. That is okay.
6. I think the picture is beautiful. You are kidding! It is terrible.
7. I am so glad to be here. We are glad, too.

5

2. That woman's beautiful. She's my wife.
3. Hello. I'm Nancy Marks. Hi. My name's Hank Stewart.
4. They're nice people. But they're so boring.
5. My daughter's in the hospital. We're sorry to hear that.
6. We're glad to meet you. It's nice to meet you, too.
7. My boyfriend's fifty-five years old. But you're only twenty-seven.

UNIT 2 THE PRESENT NEGATIVE OF *BE*

1

✓ — 2, 4, 9
3. The people are not in a house.
5. The dog is not black.
6. The man is not young.
7. The women are not sisters.
8. It is not night.
10. I am not in the picture.

2

2. California is not a country. It is a state.
3. Russia is not small. It is big.
4. Egypt and China are not people. They are countries.
5. Boston and New York are not in Canada. They are in the United States.

AK1

6. Florida is not a city. It is a state.
7. The sun is not cold. It is hot.
8. Toyotas and Fords are not airplanes. They are cars.
9. Ottawa is not the capital of the United States. Washington, D.C., is the capital of the United States. (OR Ottawa is the capital of Canada.)
10. Cigarettes are not good for people. They are bad for people.
11. The sun and the moon are not near Earth. They are far from Earth.

③

2. is	5. are	8. is not
3. is not	6. are not	9. are
4. are not	7. is	10. is not

④

2. I am right. No, you are not. You are wrong.
3. Mrs. Morris is not well. I know. Her daughter is worried about her.
4. It is time for bed. But I am not tired.
5. They are my books. No, they are not. They are my books.
6. My keys are not here. They are in my bag.
7. Maria and Ali are not in class today. They are lucky.

⑤

2. I'm afraid. Why? The dog's not (OR The dog isn't) dangerous.
3. The taxi's here. But I'm not ready.
4. You're not (OR You aren't) from the hospital. No, we're police officers.
5. They're not (OR They aren't) bad children. No, but they're bad students.
6. Your bag's on the table. It's not (OR It isn't) my bag.
7. This gift's for you. But it's not (OR it isn't) my birthday.

UNIT **THE PRESENT OF *BE*: *YES / NO* QUESTIONS**

①

3. Are you Rocky?
4. Are you and your classmates worried?
5. Is your teacher in school today?
6. We are very good students.
7. I am very thirsty.
8. Is the dog hungry?
9. Oregon is near Canada.
10. Are the children afraid of the dog?

11. Is your car red?
12. This exercise is easy.

②

2. f	5. l	8. k	11. a
3. h	6. c	9. i	12. b
4. j	7. g	10. e

③

(Some answers will vary.)

2. Are you happy? Yes, I am. (OR No, I'm not.)
3. Is your mother a student? No, she isn't.
4. Is your bedroom clean? Yes, it is. (OR No, it isn't.)
5. Are your friends from Texas? No, they're not. (OR No, they aren't.)
6. Is Carol Winston your friend? No, she isn't.
7. Are you a detective? No, I'm not.
8. Is your teacher friendly? Yes, she / he is. (OR No, she / he isn't.)
9. Are your mother and father Canadian? No, they aren't. (OR No, they're not.)
10. Are you in love? Yes, I am. (OR No, I'm not.)
11. Are your classmates middle aged? No, they're not (OR No, they aren't).

UNIT **THE PAST TENSE OF *BE*; PAST TIME MARKERS**

①

3. The shirt was $29.99.
4. The tie was $16.
5. The socks were $8.
6. The sweater was $39.
7. The coat was $145.
8. The pajamas were $19.99.
9. The shorts were $14.99.
10. The hat was $25.
11. The gloves were $22.
12. The shoes were $65.

②

3. William Shakespeare and Charles Dickens weren't Canadian.
4. Bill Clinton wasn't the first president of the United States.
5. Charlie Chaplin and Marilyn Monroe were movie stars.
6. The end of World War I wasn't in 1942.
7. *Titanic* was the name of a movie.
8. Toronto and Washington, D.C., weren't big cities 300 years ago.
9. Indira Gandhi and Napolean were famous people.

10. Nelson Mandela was a political leader.
11. Oregon and Hawaii weren't part of the United States in 1776.
12. Disneyland wasn't a famous place 100 years ago.

❸

(Answers will vary.)
2. Were you a student ten years ago? Yes, I was. (OR No, I wasn't.)
3. Were you in English class yesterday? Yes, I was. (OR No, I wasn't.)
4. Were all the students in class last week? Yes, they were. (OR No, they weren't.)
5. Was the weather nice yesterday? Yes, it was. (OR No, it wasn't.)
6. Was your teacher at work two days ago. Yes, she / he was. (OR No, she / he wasn't.)

❹

3. is	8. Is	13. Were	18. were
4. is	9. is	14. were	19. Are
5. is	10. was	15. were	20. are
6. are	11. was	16. was	
7. is	12. were	17. were	

PART Ⅱ NOUNS, ADJECTIVES, AND PREPOSITIONS; THE PRESENT PROGRESSIVE

UNIT 5 COUNT NOUNS; *A / AN*

❶

2. a	4. h	6. c	8. g
3. e	5. f	7. b	

❷

2. Tom Cruise is an actor.
3. Elizabeth II is a queen.
4. Céline Dion is a singer.
5. Neil Armstrong is an astronaut.
6. Yo Yo Ma is a musician.
7. Kristi Yamaguchi is an ice skater.
8. Sharon Stone is an actress.

❸

/z/—dictionaries, girls, lemons, sons /ɪz/—boxes, classes, houses, watches /s/—roommates, states, students, notebooks

❹

3. men	7. continents	11. universities
4. songs	8. states	12. watches
5. cities	9. countries	13. actresses
6. rivers	10. provinces	14. mountains

❺

2. 2 children, 3 children
3. 6 teeth, 7 teeth
4. 1 foot, 4 feet
5. 1 grandchild, 7 grandchildren
6. 1 person, 9 people
7. 2 sisters-in-law, 3 sisters-in-law

❻

3. They're cars.	8. They're boxes.
4. It's a house.	9. It's an oven.
5. They're books.	10. It's an egg.
6. It's an eraser.	11. They're dogs.
7. They're eyes.	12. It's a watch.

UNIT 6 DESCRIPTIVE ADJECTIVES

❶

2. big	5. expensive	8. bad
3. boring	6. dirty	9. new
4. fat	7. noisy	10. cold

❷

2. They are honest men.
3. They are tall girls.
4. They are intelligent animals.
5. Those books are expensive.
6. Eggs are white (OR brown).
7. They are good actors.
8. These watches are cheap.
9. They are interesting stories.

❸

2. It is a great book.
3. Bill Clinton is a famous politician.
4. She is a beautiful singer.
5. They are intelligent students.
6. He is an interesting man.
7. It is an expensive camera.
8. It is a long story.
9. We are good doctors.
10. You are a lucky woman.

UNIT 7 PREPOSITIONS OF PLACE

1

(Answers will vary.)

2

2. between	**5.** in	**8.** in
3. next to (OR near)	**6.** near	**9.** next to
4. near	**7.** between	**10.** near

UNIT 8 PRESENT PROGRESSIVE

1

2. e	**5.** c	**8.** f
3. b	**6.** j	**9.** h
4. a	**7.** g	**10.** i

2

3. getting	**10.** hitting
4. shining	**11.** talk
5. rain	**12.** driving
6. make	**13.** doing
7. watching	**14.** put
8. listening	**15.** begin
9. run	**16.** studying

3

3. I am (OR am not) having a good time.
4. The sun is (OR is not) shining.
5. It is (OR is not) raining.
6. It is (OR is not) getting dark.
7. I am (OR am not) listening to the radio.
8. I am (OR am not) talking on the phone.
9. I am (OR am not) sitting on a chair.
10. My best friend is (OR is not) sitting next to me.
11. My neighbors are (OR are not) making a lot of noise.
12. I am (OR am not) writing with a pencil.

4

2. is snowing	**7.** am writing
3. are skiing	**8.** are making
4. are relaxing	**9.** are enjoying
5. are sitting	**10.** is playing
6. is reading	

5

(Answers will vary.)
2. Are you wearing glasses? Yes, I am. (OR No, I'm not.)
3. Is your English teacher correcting papers? Yes, he / she is. (OR No, he / she isn't.)
4. Are you and a friend watching TV? Yes, we are. (OR No, we aren't.)
5. Are your classmates doing this exercise now? Yes, they are. (OR No, they aren't.)
6. Are your neighbors having dinner? Yes, they are. (OR No, they aren't.)
7. Is the sun shining? Yes, it is. (OR No, it isn't.)
8. Are your friends waiting for you? Yes, they are. (OR No, they aren't.)
9. Are your parents working? Yes, they are. (OR No, they aren't.)
10. Are you eating ice cream? Yes, I am. (OR No, I'm not.)
11. Is your teacher helping you with this exercise? Yes, he / she is. (OR No, he / she isn't.)
12. Are children playing outside? Yes, they are. (OR No, they aren't.)

6

2. Is she sleeping?
3. Are they playing?
4. Are they swimming?
5. Is he buying stamps?
6. Are they having a good time?
7. Is she visiting someone?
8. Are they playing tennis?
9. Is she fixing something?
10. Is he coming?
11. Are they waiting for me?
12. Is he following me?

PART III WH- QUESTIONS; POSSESSIVES; PREPOSITIONS OF TIME

UNIT 9 QUESTIONS WITH WHO, WHAT, AND WHERE

1

3. Who	**5.** Where
4. Where	**6.** What

7. Who
8. Where
9. Who

10. What
11. Where
12. What

②

3. What sports are you good at? Soccer and basketball.
4. Where are they from? Brazil.
5. Who was the woman in your garden? My best friend.
6. Where is Dallas? In Texas.
7. Where are my shoes? Under the bed.
8. What was in the bag? A sandwich.
9. Where is (OR Where's) the post office? On Park Street.
10. Who is (OR Who's) your favorite writer? Shakespeare.
11. Who are two famous presidents of the United States? Abraham Lincoln and John F. Kennedy.
12. What is (OR What's) that in the tree? A bird.

③

2. What
3. What

4. Who
5. What

6. Who
7. Where

④

2. Where's the hospital?
3. Who was John Wayne?
4. Where's Room 203?
5. Where are my keys?
6. Who were King Hussein and François Mitterand?
7. Who was (that) on the phone?
8. What are Cadillacs?
9. What's that (OR this)?
10. Where's the wastepaper basket?
11. Where were you last night?

UNIT **POSSESSIVE NOUNS AND POSSESSIVE ADJECTIVES; QUESTIONS WITH *WHOSE***

①

2. e
3. a

4. b
5. f

6. i
7. g

8. h
9. d

②

2. your, their
3. her, his
4. our, their

5. my, her
6. your, his, my (OR our), Her

③

2. He, His
3. She, her
4. They, Their, their, It
5. We, Our

6. I, my
7. He, His
8. We, Our, Its, It
9. Their, They, They

④

3. His last name is Barba.
4. He's a grandfather.
5. Their names are Lydia and Daphne.
6. She's twelve years old.
7. Her hair is long.
8. His dogs are always outside.
9. Her eyes are blue.
10. She's afraid of the dogs.
11. They were with their grandfather yesterday.
12. He was with his dogs.
13. Their food was in the garage.
14. They were in the garage.
15. Their friends were not with them today.
16. They were happy to be with their grandfather.

⑤

3. Whose eggs are these?
4. Whose bananas are these?
5. Whose bread is this?
6. Whose potatoes are these?
7. Whose cake is this?
8. Whose milk is this?
9. Whose orange juice is this?
10. Whose potato chips are these?
11. Whose carrots are these?
12. Whose bag is this?

⑥

3. Winston's
4. men's
5. husband's
6. babies'
7. girls' school

8. brothers'
9. son's
10. doctor's
11. teacher's
12. teachers'

⑦

2. Mrs. Simpson's
3. Mary Rose's
4. Nora's
5. Bill's

6. Joe Mott's
7. Dr. Lin's
8. Maria Lico's
9. Tom Cho's

UNIT **QUESTIONS WITH *WHEN* AND *WHAT* + NOUN; PREPOSITIONS; ORDINAL NUMBERS**

** 1**

At—night; half past six
In—the morning; the summer; the evening; 1888;
    May; the spring
On—June 30th; December 3rd; January 15, 2000;
    Thursday

2

2. It's at 2:30.
3. It's at nine o'clock in the morning.
4. It's on Friday.
5. It's on Saturday.
6. It's at eight o'clock.
7. No, it's in the afternoon.
8. It's at three o'clock.
9. No, it's in the evening.

3

3. what is the date? (OR what day is it?)
4. what time is it?
5. when is it?
6. when is it?
7. what time is it? (OR when is it?)
8. when is it open?
9. when is your birthday? (OR what day is your birthday?)

4

3. 9th	8. 80th
4. 12th	9. 95th
5. 23rd	10. 101st
6. 51st	11. 116th
7. 72nd	12. 200th

5

3. third	8. forty-seventh
4. eleventh	9. sixty-sixth
5. fifteenth	10. eighty-second
6. twentieth	11. ninety-ninth
7. thirty-first	12. one hundred and third

6

2. Twenty-third Street and First Avenue
3. Forty-third Street and Tenth Avenue
4. Fifty-second Street and Sixth Avenue
5. Eighty-sixth Street and Fifth Avenue
6. Fourteenth Street and Eighth Avenue
7. Sixty-ninth Street and Second Avenue

** 7**

2. It's on January thirty-first.
3. It's on January tenth.
4. It's on February fifth.
5. It's on January twentieth.
6. It's on February ninth.
7. It's on January third.
8. It's on February eighteenth.
9. It's on January first.
10. It's on February twenty-second.

UNIT **QUESTIONS WITH *WHO*, *WHOM*, AND *WHY*; *WH-* QUESTIONS AND THE PRESENT PROGRESSIVE**

1

2. A pineapple.
3. They are waiting.
4. An old woman.
5. In a store.
6. A dress.
7. Behind Doug. (OR In front of the old woman.)

2

2. Where are you hiding the gift?
3. Who is knocking on the door?
4. What are your children wearing?
5. Who is she waiting for?
6. What are you looking for?
7. Why are they shouting?
8. Where are they going?
9. Why is she sending him a gift?
10. What are you doing?

3

2. What are you doing?
3. Why are you leaving so early?
4. What are you looking for?
5. Where are you hiding the gift?
6. Who is knocking on the door?
7. What are your children wearing?
8. Who is she waiting for?
9. Where are they going?
10. Why is she sending him a gift?

4

2. a	4. a	6. b
3. b	5. b	7. a

5

2. What are you reading?
3. What are they eating?
4. What is he cooking?
5. Who is coming?
6. Why are you going to bed?
7. Where are you going?
8. Why are you selling it?
9. Where are they swimming?
10. What are you watching?
11. Who are they watching?
12. Who is she dating?

PART IV THE SIMPLE PRESENT TENSE

UNIT SIMPLE PRESENT TENSE: AFFIRMATIVE AND NEGATIVE STATEMENTS

1

2. They're secretaries.
3. He's a pilot.
4. She's a professor.
5. They're flight attendants.
6. You're a cook.
7. You're a salesperson.
8. She's a doctor.

2

2. teaches	5. plays	8. paint
3. sings	6. manages	9. washes
4. dances	7. collect	10. fight

3

3. doesn't	5. don't	7. don't	9. don't
4. doesn't	6. doesn't	8. don't	10. don't

4

2. take	10. lives	18. doesn't come
3. goes	11. has	19. isn't
4. has	12. is	20. helps
5. live	13. doesn't have	21. go
6. don't live	14. live	22. don't have
7. have	15. studies	23. try
8. don't live	16. works	24. don't get
9. is	17. leaves	

5

2. Water doesn't boil at 90° C. It boils at 100° C.
3. Water doesn't freeze at 5° C. It freezes at 0° C.
4. The Sun doesn't go around the Earth. The Earth goes around the Sun.
5. Penguins don't come from the Arctic. They come from the Antarctic.
6. Cows don't eat meat. They eat grass.
7. China doesn't have a small population. It has a big population.
8. Deserts don't have a lot of water. They have a lot of sand.
9. Elephants don't have small ears. They have big ears.
10. Egypt doesn't have a cold climate. It has a hot climate.
11. The sun doesn't shine at night. It shines during the day.
12. Mice don't run after cats. Cats run after mice.

UNIT 14 SIMPLE PRESENT TENSE: *YES / NO* QUESTIONS AND SHORT ANSWERS

1

2. a	5. c	8. a	11. d
3. d	6. b	9. c	12. c
4. a	7. d	10. b	

2

2. f	4. g	6. a	8. d
3. c	5. b	7. h	

3

3. Yes, she does.	7. No, she doesn't.
4. No, she doesn't.	8. Yes, he does.
5. Yes, they do.	9. No, they don't.
6. Yes, he does.	10. Yes, they do.

4

2. Does your roommate like your girlfriend?
3. Does the teacher wear glasses?
4. Does Mr. Flagg have a car?
5. Do Jack and Jill sleep until ten o'clock?
6. Does Peter eat fast?
7. Does she leave for work at the same time every day?
8. Does the dog eat two times a day?
9. Does the doctor have your telephone number?
10. Do football players play in the summer?

11. Who has my keys?
12. Who does the doctor want to see first?

5

2. Does she have
3. Do they like
4. Do you live
5. Does he know
6. Do you want
7. Do you have

8. Does it belong
9. Do you like
10. Do you know
11. Do they work
12. Does he come

UNIT **15** SIMPLE PRESENT TENSE:
WH- QUESTIONS

1

3. Where
4. What
5. Who
6. What time (OR When)
7. Who

8. Where
9. When
10. Why
11. What time (OR When)
12. When

2

2. What do you have for breakfast? Cereal.
3. What time does your husband get up? At 6:00.
4. Who corrects your homework? My teacher.
5. Where does Rosita work? At City Central Bank.
6. When do you and your family go on vacation? In August.
7. What do you wear to work? A suit and tie.
8. Why do you need more money? Because I want to buy a sweatshirt.
9. What time do the kids eat lunch? At noon.
10. When does the mail come? In the morning.
11. Where does Doug meet his friends? At his school.
12. Who does Milt visit on Sundays? His parents.

3

2. What time (OR When)
3. Who
4. Where
5. What
6. When

7. Where
8. Who
9. Why
10. What

4

2. Why do you drive your children to school?
3. What do pilots do?
4. What time (OR When) does the bank open?
5. Why are you studying?
6. Where do your brothers live?
7. Who (usually) does the shopping?
8. When do American children start school?
9. Who lives in the big white house?
10. What do you do on the weekend?

UNIT **16** SIMPLE PRESENT TENSE AND
THIS / THAT / THESE / THOSE

1

2. This is a gift for you.
3. This hamburger is terrible. These potatoes are awful, too.
4. This television is heavy. This bookcase is heavy, too.
5. Brenda, this is Tim.
6. These shoes are only $35.
7. This is a great party.
8. These are beautiful earrings. This bracelet is nice, too.
9. These cookies are for you.
10. These are my parents.

2

2. What's this?
3. What's this?
4. What's this?
5. What are these?
6. What are these?

7. What's this?
8. What are these?
9. What are these?
10. What's this?

3

2. that
3. those
4. those
5. Those

6. that
7. that
8. that
9. that

10. those
11. those
12. those

4

2. that
3. this
4. this

5. those
6. These
7. those

8. That
9. These
10. that

UNIT **17** SIMPLE PRESENT TENSE AND
ONE / ONES AND *IT*

1

2. g
3. a

4. h
5. b

6. c
7. f

8. e

2

2. No, I prefer the brown ones.
3. The one in the corner?
4. No, only the ones in the bowl.
5. This one is terrible.
6. No, but there's one about a mile away.
7. The ones on the kitchen table.
8. No, but Carla wants one.
9. I like it, too.
10. The other ones are better.
11. No, give me the ones over there.
12. But the one on Fifth Street costs less.
13. Do you want the gold earrings OR the silver ones?
14. It is on the table near the door.

PART V THE SIMPLE PAST TENSE

UNIT **18** **SIMPLE PAST TENSE: REGULAR VERBS—AFFIRMATIVE AND NEGATIVE STATEMENTS**

1

2. i   4. e   6. b   8. f
3. a   5. g   7. c   9. h

2

2. Last   4. Yesterday   6. yesterday
3. Last   5. yesterday   7. last

3

2. Eric traveled to Poland _____ years ago.
3. Eric visited his college roommate _____ months ago.
4. Eric called his parents _____ days ago.
5. Eric talked to his boss about a raise _____ days ago.
6. Eric graduated from college _____ years ago.
7. Eric moved to Georgia _____ months ago.
8. Eric played tennis _____ days ago.
9. Eric studied Polish _____ years ago.
10. Eric's grandfather died _____ months ago.

4

2. They played basketball.
3. She washed her clothes.
4. They studied.
5. He worked in his garden.
6. She prepared dinner at 6:00.
7. Anna talked to her daughter.
8. They traveled to France.
9. The bank closed at 3:00 P.M.
10. They watched television.

5

2. invited, didn't invite
3. cleaned, didn't clean
4. talked, didn't talk
5. called, didn't call
6. watched, didn't watch
7. returned, didn't return
8. painted, didn't paint
9. cooked, didn't cook
10. studied, didn't study

6

2. am thinking   13. speak
3. think   14. don't speak
4. is shining   15. laughs
5. are singing   16. invited
6. rained   17. listened
7. stayed   18. danced
8. didn't go   19. enjoyed
9. washed   20. am cooking
10. cleaned   21. need
11. played   22. don't want
12. comes   23. know

UNIT **19** **SIMPLE PAST TENSE: IRREGULAR VERBS—AFFIRMATIVE AND NEGATIVE STATEMENTS**

1

3. *put*, irregular, put
4. *had*, irregular, have
5. *brushed*, regular, brush
6. *left*, irregular, leave
7. *arrived*, regular, arrive
8. *began*, irregular, begin
9. *learned*, regular, learn
10. *finished*, regular, finish
11. *met*, irregular, meet
12. *ate*, irregular, eat
13. *went*, irregular, go
14. *stayed*, regular, stay

❷

2. drank	7. stole	12. came
3. left	8. found	13. read
4. met	9. drove	14. sent
5. spoke	10. saw	15. forgot
6. went	11. brought	

❸

(Probable answers)

2. I didn't eat three kilos of oranges for breakfast yesterday morning.
3. I didn't sleep twenty-one hours yesterday.
4. I didn't bring a horse to English class two weeks ago.
5. I didn't go to the moon last month.
6. I didn't meet the leader of my country last night.
7. I didn't find $10,000 in a brown paper bag yesterday.
8. I didn't do this exercise two years ago.
9. I didn't swim thirty kilometers yesterday.
10. I didn't speak English perfectly ten years ago.

❹

2. didn't get	14. bought
3. got	15. didn't buy
4. went	16. came
5. met	17. made
6. went	18. didn't have
7. didn't see	19. drove
8. didn't have	20. saw
9. closed	21. invited
10. ate	22. didn't eat
11. took	23. watched
12. stayed	24. didn't leave
13. looked	

UNIT **SIMPLE PAST TENSE: *YES / NO* AND *WH-* QUESTIONS**

❶

2. Yes, they did.	6. No, they didn't.
3. No, she didn't.	7. No, he didn't.
4. Yes, he did.	8. No, they didn't.
5. Yes, she did.	9. Yes, he did.

❷

2. Did you do all the homework? Yes, I did. (OR No, I didn't.)
3. Did you take a bath this morning? Yes, I did. (OR No, I didn't.)
4. Did your best friend come over to your house last night? Yes, he / she did. (OR No, he / she didn't.)

5. Did you go to bed early last night? Yes, I did. (OR No, I didn't.)
6. Did your English teacher teach you new grammar last week? Yes, he / she did. (OR No, he / she didn't.)
7. Did you visit the United States ten years ago? Yes, I did. (OR No, I didn't.)
8. Did your mother and father get married a long time ago? Yes, they did. (OR No, they didn't.)
9. Did you watch television last night? Yes, I did. (OR No, I didn't.)

❸

3. Did you buy food for dinner?
4. got
5. Did you meet Glen for lunch?
6. ate
7. Did you write a letter to Rena?
8. mailed
9. Did you go to the bank?
10. deposited
11. Did you return the book to the library?
12. took
13. Did you look for a birthday present for Jane?
14. bought
15. Did you call the doctor?
16. said
17. Did you bake some cookies?
18. had
19. Did you pick the children up at 4:00?
20. forgot

❹

2. i	5. g	8. h
3. c	6. b	9. d
4. a	7. e	

❺

2. When did a human being walk on the moon for the first time? In 1969.
3. What did William Shakespeare write? Plays like *Romeo and Juliet*.
4. Where did the Olympic Games start? In Greece.
5. Why did many people go to California in 1849? They wanted to find gold.
6. How long did John F. Kennedy live in the White House? Almost three years.
7. What did Alfred Hitchcock make? Movies.
8. Why did the Chinese build the Great Wall? They wanted to keep foreigners out of the country.
9. How long did World War II last in Europe? About six years.
10. When did Christopher Columbus discover America? In 1492.

6

2. Who gave
3. Who did you see
4. Who called?
5. Who wrote
6. Who took

7. Who did she send
8. Who cleaned
9. Who did she marry?
10. Who did they stay

7

2. Who did you go with? (OR Who went with you?)
3. What time (OR When) did you leave your home?
4. What time (OR When) did the movie start?
5. Why did you leave your house so early?
6. Where did you eat? (OR Where did you have dinner?)
7. Where did you meet your friend?
8. What did you eat (OR have)?
9. Who saw you?
10. Why did you talk to the manager?
11. Where did you go after dinner?
12. What did you see?
13. Where did you see the movie?

PART **VI** IMPERATIVES; SUGGESTIONS; *THERE IS / THERE ARE*

UNIT **21** IMPERATIVES; SUGGESTIONS WITH *LET'S, WHY DON'T WE . . . ?; WHY DON'T YOU . . . ?*

1

2. e	5. a	8. j
3. b	6. i	9. f
4. c	7. g	10. h

2

3. Clean	7. Don't be	11. Don't use
4. Don't talk	8. Don't tell	12. Don't touch
5. Don't buy	9. Study	
6. Ask	10. Give	

3

2. Get off	5. Walk (OR Go)
3. Go (OR Walk)	6. make
4. turn	7. Ring

4

2. b	5. a	8. a
3. b	6. a	9. a
4. a	7. b	10. b

5

2. Let's get something to eat.
3. Let's go swimming.
4. Let's not invite her to the party.
5. Why don't we go out and look for him?
6. Why don't we go inside?
7. Why don't we leave?

6

2. e
3. b
4. a
5. d
6. *(Possible answer)* Why don't you turn on the TV?
7. *(Possible answer)* Why don't you watch movies in English?
8. *(Possible answer)* Why don't you take an aspirin?

UNIT **22** SUBJECT AND OBJECT PRONOUNS; DIRECT AND INDIRECT OBJECTS

1

2. his daughter	5. my ice cream
3. page 104	6. five stamps
4. the teacher	

2

| 2. you | 4. it | 6. it | 8. us |
| 3. me | 5. her | 7. them | |

3

1. me	4. she, her	7. their, them
2. you	5. its, it	
3. his	6. we, us	

4

2. you	6. him	10. her
3. him	7. us	11. her
4. her	8. them	12. you
5. me	9. them	

5

2. She loves him.
3. They love us.
4. We love them.
5. Tell me the answer.
6. Show her the paper.
7. Take them some flowers.
8. Send me a postcard.

6

2. It, it
3. she, her
4. him, He
5. I, me
6. they, them
7. we, us
8. you

7

2. e
3. g
4. h
5. c
6. b
7. a
8. d

8

2. answers, you
3. this check, me
4. this joke, Bill
5. the salt and pepper, me
6. the story, me
7. your passport, me
8. the information, you

9

2. He gave Bob a CD.
3. He gave his brother a video game.
4. He gave Marge some earrings.
6. He gave a book to Bill.
7. He gave some sunglasses to his cousin.
8. He gave a ring to his girlfriend.

10

2. it to them
3. them to her
4. them to me
5. it to me
6. it to them

11

2. I lent some money to him.
3. The man is showing something to the women.
4. She always gives them some help.
5. Did you tell him the answer?
6. I send all my friends birthday cards.
7. Throw the ball to me.
8. You didn't explain this sentence to us.
9. He owes me fifty dollars.

UNIT **THERE IS / THERE ARE /**
IS THERE . . . ? /
ARE THERE . . . ?

1

2. There is
3. there are
4. There is
5. there are
6. There are
7. there is
8. There are
9. There is
10. there is

2

2. There is a knife on the table.
3. There are two cars in the garage.
4. There are flowers in the garden.
5. There is a dog under the bed.
6. There is a box between the two chairs.
7. There is a picture on the wall.
8. There are five books on the floor.
9. There are seven rooms in this house.

3

3. There is a clock in the tree.
4. There is a bicycle in the tree.
5. There is a bed in the tree.
6. There are televisions in the tree.
7. There are balls in the tree.
8. There are hats in the tree.
9. There are books in the tree.
10. There are cups in the tree.
11. There are keys in the tree.
12. There are pens in the tree.
13. There are eggs in the tree.

4

3. There are two beds in every room.
4. There are two closets in every room.
5. There isn't a telephone in every room.
6. There is a television in every room.
7. There is an air conditioner in every room.
8. There isn't a refrigerator in every room.
9. There isn't a swimming pool at the hotel.
10. There are two restaurants at the hotel.
11. There are four tennis courts at the hotel.
12. There aren't tourist shops at the hotel.
13. There are two parking lots at the hotel.

5

3. There are two banks. They are on Main Street.
4. There are three clothing stores. They aren't very expensive.
5. There aren't any bookstores.
6. There are four drugstores. They're small.
7. There are three gas stations. They are in the center of town.
8. There aren't any hospitals.
9. There aren't any movie theaters.
10. There are two restaurants. They are open for lunch and dinner.
11. There are three schools. They aren't far from Main Street.
12. There are two supermarkets. They are big.
13. There aren't any swimming pools.

6

2. Yes, there are.
3. Yes, there are.
4. No, there aren't.
5. No, there aren't.
6. No, there aren't.
7. Yes, there are.
8. No, there aren't.
9. No, there aren't.

7

2. Are there many elephants in India? Yes, there are.
3. Is there a desert in Canada? No, there isn't.
4. Are there camels in Saudi Arabia? Yes, there are.
5. Is there a long river in the Sahara Desert? No, there isn't.
6. Are there many lions in Russia? No, there aren't.
7. Are there mountains in Kenya? Yes, there are.
8. Are there many people in Antarctica? No, there aren't.
9. Is there a big city in Thailand? Yes, there is.
10. Is there a monkey in your garden? No, there isn't.

UNIT **NUMBERS, QUANTIFIERS, AND QUESTIONS WITH HOW MANY . . . ?**

1

2. a
3. a
4. b
5. b
6. a
7. a
8. b
9. a

2

3. There aren't any students from Russia.
4. There are many students from Japan.
5. There are many students from Venezuela.
6. There is a student from Turkey.
7. There aren't any students from Morocco.
8. There is a student from Greece.
9. There are a few students from Mexico.
10. There aren't any students from Indonesia.
11. There are a few students from China.
12. There aren't any students from France.

3

2. How many telephones (OR clocks) (OR bicycles) (OR beds) are there?
3. How many balls are there?
4. How many suitcases are there?
5. How many hats are there?
6. How many books are there?
7. How many cups are there?
8. How many keys are there?
9. How many pens are there?
10. How many eggs are there?

PART VII REVIEW OF THE SIMPLE PRESENT TENSE AND THE PRESENT PROGRESSIVE

UNIT **PRESENT AND PRESENT PROGRESSIVE; HOW OFTEN . . . ?; ADVERBS AND EXPRESSIONS OF FREQUENCY**

1

3, 4, 7, 8, and 9 are true.

2

3. I rarely practice in the middle of the night.
4. I seldom fight with customers.
5. I often drive at night.
6. I am always careful.
7. I almost always find the problem with the car.
8. I never put lemon in milk.
9. I am bored once in a while
10. The hospital is open every day.
11. I almost never wear a suit and tie to work.
12. We are frequently away from home for three OR four days at a time.

3

2. How often does Donna play basketball? She frequently plays basketball.
3. How often does David swim? He never swims.
4. How often do Barbara and Ed play basketball? They never play basketball.
5. How often does Ed jog? He often jogs.

6. How often does Barbara swim? She swims three times a week.
7. How often do Barbara and David jog? They rarely jog.
8. How often do Ed and George swim? They swim once OR twice a week.
9. How often do George and David play basketball? They play basketball almost every day.
10. How often does George jog? He almost never jogs.
11. How often do you jog?
12. How often do you do exercises?

4

2. a	5. c	8. h	11. j
3. b	6. f	9. l	12. g
4. e	7. k	10. d	

5

2. drives, is (OR 's) driving a bus
3. fixes cars, is (OR 's) fixing cars
4. serves food, is (OR 's) serving food
5. paint pictures, are (OR 're) painting pictures
6. do experiments, (OR 're) doing experiments
7. write articles, are (OR 're) writing articles
8. cuts meat, is (OR 's) cutting meat
9. counts money, is (OR 's) counting money
10. bake bread and cake, are (OR 're) baking bread and cake
11. waters plants and flowers, is (OR 's) watering plants and flowers
12. feeds animals, is (OR 's) feeding animals

6

2. Are you doing
3. am cutting
4. Do you prepare
5. eat
6. do you have
7. eat
8. go
9. are getting
10. doesn't go
11. Do your kids go
12. don't stay up
13. get up
14. are
15. does your daughter do
16. Does she watch
17. practices
18. is practicing
19. does she practice
20. Does she play
21. are
22. am working
23. is
24. Do you have

UNIT NON-ACTION VERBS

1

3. <u>have</u>, non-action verb
4. <u>is having</u>, action verb
5. <u>belongs</u>, non-action verb
6. <u>need</u>, non-action verb

7. <u>like</u>, non-action verb
8. <u>come</u>, action verb
9. <u>smell</u>, non-action verb
10. <u>are . . . smelling</u>, action verb
11. <u>do</u>, action verb
12. <u>hate</u>, non-action verb
13. <u>know</u>, non-action verb
14. <u>are running</u>, action verb

2

2. a	6. b	10. a	14. a
3. b	7. a	11. a	
4. a	8. b	12. b	
5. a	9. a	13. b	

3

2. don't care
3. Do you want
4. is playing
5. don't know
6. don't have
7. is raining
8. have
9. don't have
10. don't need
11. like
12. wants
13. don't think
14. has
15. is doing
16. hear
17. is talking
18. is talking
19. doesn't understand
20. is getting
21. do you know
22. know
23. don't know

UNIT VERBS PLUS NOUNS, GERUNDS, AND INFINITIVES

1

2. i	4. a	6. e	8. g
3. b	5. c	7. h	9. f

2

2. Milt is good at fixing things.
3. Pete enjoys fishing.
4. Elenore is interested in collecting stamps.
5. Norma enjoys gardening.
6. Carol is good at riding horses.
7. Lulu is interested in learning Spanish.
8. Yoko is good at cooking.

3

2. to swim (OR swimming)
3. to help
4. to talk
5. to move
6. to be
7. to receive (OR receiving)
8. to study (OR studying)
9. to relax
10. studying

UNIT POSSESSIVE ADJECTIVES AND POSSESSIVE PRONOUNS

1

3. correct
4. correct
5. Please bring me my car.
6. Where is her car?
7. correct
8. correct
9. We need our car.
10. Their car is expensive.
11. correct
12. Why do you want your car?

2

2. Mine	5. Yours	8. hers
3. his	6. theirs	9. Theirs
4. ours	7. his	10. ours

3

2. my, yours, mine	5. Their, their, theirs
3. hers, hers	6. his, his
4. our, ours	

PART VIII REVIEW OF THE SIMPLE PAST TENSE; NEGATIVE QUESTIONS; THE FUTURE

UNIT REVIEW OF THE SIMPLE PAST TENSE; NEGATIVE QUESTIONS

1

2. made	5. didn't have	8. didn't eat
3. left	6. didn't play	9. watched
4. were	7. bought	

2

2. No, they weren't. (OR Yes, they were.)
3. Yes, I did. (OR No, I didn't.)
4. Yes, he was. (OR No, he wasn't.)
5. Yes, it was. (OR No, it wasn't.)
6. Yes, I did. (OR No, I didn't.)
7. Yes, I was. (OR No, I wasn't.)
8. No, they didn't. (OR Yes, they did.)
9. Yes, we did. (OR No, we didn't.)
10. Yes, it was. (OR No, it wasn't.)
11. Yes, he / she did. (OR No, he / she didn't.)
12. Yes, I was. (OR No, I wasn't.)

3

2. Were they on sale? Yes, they were only $25.
3. Were you at home last night? No, I was at the library.
4. Were the guests late for the party? No, they were all on time.
5. Was it warm in Australia? The weather was beautiful every day.
6. Was the movie good? It was okay.
7. Were the people at the party friendly? Most of them were very nice.
8. Was he there? No, he was at a meeting.

4

2. Didn't you eat	5. Didn't you like
3. Weren't you	6. Wasn't
4. Didn't it rain	7. Didn't you see

UNIT 30 WH- QUESTIONS IN THE SIMPLE PAST TENSE

1

2. b	5. a	8. b
3. a	6. a	9. b
4. b	7. b	10. a

2

2. f, were	5. a, were	8. l, did	11. g, did
3. i, did	6. c, did	9. d, was	12. h, were
4. b, was	7. j, was	10. k, was	

3

2. were you
3. was it
4. were they afraid
5. was the score
6. was the name of the store
7. were they born
8. were they here
9. were you with (OR was with you)
10. was Eleanor Roosevelt

UNIT *BE GOING TO* FOR THE FUTURE;
FUTURE AND PAST TIME MARKERS

❶

2. this evening
3. next month
4. tomorrow morning
5. next week
6. tonight
7. tomorrow night (OR this week)

❷

2. in two weeks
3. in three days
4. in two months
5. in ten minutes

❸

(Answers will vary.)

❹

(Possible answers)
I am (OR am not) going to study.
I am (OR am not) going to go shopping.
I am (OR am not) going to clean.
I am (OR am not) going to watch TV.
I am (OR am not) going to go out with friends.
I am (OR am not) going to listen to music.
I am (OR am not) going to visit relatives.
I am (OR am not) going to talk on the telephone.
I am (OR am not) going to take a shower.
I am (OR am not) going to write a letter.
I am (OR am not) going to read a newspaper.
I am (OR am not) going to stay home.

❺

(Possible answers)
2. She's going to study.
3. They're going to write letters.
4. They're going to ski.
5. He's going to listen to music.
6. He's going to take pictures.

❻

2. She isn't going to take
3. She isn't going to take
4. They aren't going to play
5. They aren't going to watch
6. I'm not going to eat
7. We aren't going to swim
8. He isn't going to see
9. I'm not going to wake up
10. He isn't going to deliver

❼

2. Who is going to cook tonight?
3. When is dinner going to be ready?
4. Why is he going to cook so much food?
5. How long is he going to need to cook the dinner?
6. Who is going to come?
7. How is he going to cook the lamb?
8. Where are all of your guests going to sit?
9. What are you going to do?
10. How long are your guests going to stay?

❽

2. What is he going to make?
3. Why is he going to cook so much food?
4. How is he going to cook the lamb?
5. Who is going to come?
6. How long is he going to need to cook the dinner?
7. What are you going to do?
8. When is dinner going to be ready?
9. How long are your guests going to stay?
10. Where are all of your guests going to sit?

❾

3. 'm doing, now
4. 're . . . going, future
5. 's leaving, future
6. Are . . . doing, now
7. Is . . . coming, future
8. are . . . listening, now
9. are . . . going, now
10. is . . . waiting, now

❿

2. They are flying to London at 7:30 on May 8.
3. They are arriving in London at 6:45 A.M. on May 9.
4. They are staying at the London Regency Hotel on May 9 and 10.
5. They are visiting Buckingham Palace at 2 P.M. on May 9.
6. They are having tea at the Ritz Hotel at 4:30 on May 9.
7. They are going to the theater at 7:30 on May 9.
8. They are going on a tour of central London at 9:00 A.M. on May 10.
9. They are eating lunch at a typical English pub at twelve o'clock on May 10.
10. They are leaving for Scotland at 8:00 A.M. on May 11.

11

2. Are you going to the movies this weekend? Yes, I am. (OR No, I'm not.)
3. Are you taking a trip next week? Yes, I am. (OR No, I'm not.)
4. Can your friend leave in two hours? Yes, he / she can. (OR No, he / she can't.)
5. Are your classmates meeting you tonight? Yes, they are. (OR No, they aren't.)
6. Is your mother driving to work tomorrow? Yes, she is. (OR No, she isn't.)
7. Is your father taking an English class next year? Yes, he is. (OR No, he isn't.)
8. Are your neighbors doing anything this weekend? Yes, they are. (OR No, they aren't.)
9. Are you and your friends playing cards next Saturday? Yes, we are. (OR No, we aren't.)
10. Can your parents call your teacher tonight? Yes, they can. (OR No, they can't.)

12

2. When are you leaving?
3. How are you getting there? (OR How are you going?)
4. Why are you driving?
5. How long are you staying?
6. Who are you going with?
7. What are you taking?

UNIT 32 WILL FOR THE FUTURE

1

2. I'll get you some water.
3. I'll help you.
4. I'll buy you some.
5. I'll turn on the air conditioner.
6. I'll make you a sandwich.
7. I'll get you some aspirin.
8. I'll drive you.
9. I'll wash them.

2

2. He won't lose his job.
3. I'll have a cup of coffee.
4. It'll rain this evening.
5. She won't be happy.
6. They'll have a good time.
7. You won't like it.

3

2. a	4. a	6. b	8. a
3. b	5. a	7. b	9. b

4

2. I won't leave late.
3. It won't be hot.
4. Coffee won't cost more.
5. The dishes won't be dirty.
6. We won't come before seven o'clock.
7. Mr. and Mrs. McNamara won't buy a new car.
8. I won't make many eggs.
9. Valerie won't lose the game.
10. The parking lot won't be full.

5

2. Will I be	11. won't be
3. will marry	12. will bother
4. will I meet	13. won't like
5. will be	14. Will our home have
6. Will she love	15. won't leave
7. will we meet	16. won't bother
8. won't have	17. will become
9. will be	18. Will that make
10. will I be	

PART NOUNS, ARTICLES, AND QUANTIFIERS; MODALS I

UNIT 33 COUNT AND NON-COUNT NOUNS AND QUANTIFIERS

1

2. 5	6. 8	10. 4	14. 8
3. 7	7. 4	11. 5	15. 3
4. 1	8. 1	12. 7	
5. 9	9. 8	13. 2	

2

Count Nouns—eggs, vegetables, napkins, bags, potato chips, toothbrushes
Non-Count Nouns—ice cream, fruit, milk, rice, food, bread, fish

3

Count Nouns—a student, some teeth, some children, some friends, an animal, some people, an uncle, a television, some questions, a computer
Non-Count Nouns—some water, some paper, some homework, some advice, some traffic, some furniture, some money, some information, some rain, some oil

4

2. a	5. a	8. b	11. b
3. a	6. a	9. a	
4. b	7. a	10. a	

5

2. A	4. the	6. the, a	8. a, a
3. the	5. a	7. the, the	

6

3. He bought some orange juice.
4. He didn't buy any lemons.
5. He bought a newspaper.
6. He didn't buy any bread.
7. He didn't buy any onions.
8. He didn't buy a toothbrush.
9. He bought some potatoes.
10. He didn't buy any lettuce.
11. He didn't buy any carrots.
12. He bought some butter.
13. He bought some milk.
14. He bought some eggs.

7

(Answers will vary.)
a lot of / any—food in my refrigerator, money in
my pocket, books next to my bed, shirts in my
closet, friends, free time, children, work to do
today, questions for my teacher, jewelry, medicine
in my bathroom, problems with English
grammar, photographs in my wallet, ice cream at
home
a little / much—cheese in my pocket, food in my
refrigerator, money in my pocket, free time, work
to do today, jewelry, medicine in my bathroom,
ice cream at home
a few / many—books next to my bed, shirts in my
closet, friends, children, questions for my teacher,
problems with English grammar, photographs in
my wallet

UNIT **QUESTIONS WITH *ANY* / *SOME* /
HOW MUCH / *HOW MANY*;
QUANTIFIERS; CONTAINERS**

1

2. d	5. g	8. e	11. j
3. a	6. h	9. l	12. i
4. c	7. f	10. k	

2

3. One carton.	6. One.	9. One tube.
4. Two heads.	7. Four.	10. Two.
5. Three.	8. Three bars.	

3

4. Is there any furniture in your home? Yes,
   there is. (OR No, there isn't.)
5. Are there any clothes in your closet? Yes,
   there are. (OR No, there aren't.)
6. Is there any money under your bed? Yes, there
   is. (OR No, there isn't.)
7. Is there an alarm clock next to your bed? Yes,
   there is. (OR No, there isn't.)
8. Is there any snow outside your home? Yes,
   there is. (OR No, there isn't.)
9. Is there a sink in your bathroom? Yes, there is.
   (OR No, there isn't.)
10. Are there any dishes in your kitchen sink? Yes,
    there are. (OR No, there aren't.)
11. Are there any pictures in your bedroom? Yes,
    there are. (OR No, there aren't.)
12. Is there any candy in your home? Yes, there
    is. (OR No, there isn't.)
13. Is there a window in your kitchen? Yes, there
    is. (OR No, there isn't.)
14. Is there a television in your living room? Yes,
    there is. (OR No, there isn't.)

4

3. How much flour do you need?
4. How much sugar do you have?
5. How many bananas do you want?
6. How many oranges do you want?
7. How much cereal do you need?
8. How many potatoes do you need?
9. How much milk do you want?
10. How many roses do you want?
11. How many cookies do you have?
12. How much money do you have?

5

2. There are too many days.
3. There are too many numbers.
4. There is too much water.
5. There is too much furniture.
6. There is too much food.
7. There are too many birds.
8. There is too much shampoo.
9. There are not enough batteries.
10. There is not enough toothpaste.
11. There is not enough air.
12. There are not enough chairs.

6

3. There were too few people for two teams.
4. We had too little paper for everyone in the class.
5. There was too little food for fifteen people.
6. You have too little information.
7. There are too many bedrooms in that apartment.
8. We had too little time for that test.
9. There are too few bananas for a banana cake.
10. There are too few sales people at that store.

7

2. b	5. a	8. a
3. a	6. b	9. b
4. b	7. b	10. a

UNIT 35 *CAN* AND *COULD* FOR ABILITY AND POSSIBILITY; *MAY I*, *CAN I*, AND *COULD I* FOR POLITE REQUESTS

1

2. secretary
3. driver
4. summer camp worker

2

4. He can drive and lift 100 pounds.
5. He can type and speak Spanish.
6. She can play the guitar and draw.
7. He can't drive, and he can't lift 100 pounds.
8. She can type, but she can't speak Spanish.
9. She can lift 100 pounds, but she can't drive.
10. He can draw, but he can't play the guitar.
11. She can't draw, and she can't play the guitar.
12. He can't type, and he can't speak Spanish.

3

2. Can your mother lift 100 pounds? Yes, she can. (OR No, she can't.)
3. Can your father play the guitar? Yes, he can. (OR No, he can't.)
4. Can your best friend ride a horse? Yes, he / she can. (OR No, he / she can't.)
5. Can your parents speak Spanish? Yes, they can. (OR No, they can't.)
6. Can you swim? Yes, I can. (OR No, I can't.)
7. Can you type? Yes, I can. (OR No, I can't.)

4

2. could practice	7. couldn't find
3. couldn't go	8. could hear
4. couldn't understand	9. couldn't go
5. couldn't eat	10. could do
6. could play	

5

2. Can I (OR May I) open the window?
3. Can I (OR May I) use the telephone?
4. Can I (OR May I) get a ride (with you)?
5. Can I (OR May I) use (OR borrow) your eraser?
6. Can I (OR May I) have a drink of water?
7. Can I (OR May I) ask you a question?
8. Can I (OR May I) sit at the empty table in the corner?

UNIT 36 *MAY* OR *MIGHT* FOR POSSIBILITY

1

3. permission	7. possibility
4. possibility	8. permission
5. possibility	9. possibility
6. permission	10. permission

2

2. We may (OR might) come by taxi.
3. He may (OR might) not want to come.
4. They may (OR might) study.
5. The store may (OR might) be closed.
6. She may (OR might) not finish the work by Friday.
7. The dog may (OR might) come home.
8. You may (OR might) not like that kind of food.
9. I may (OR might) not leave before seven o'clock.
10. The cookies may (OR might) not taste good.

3

3. may	5. will	7. may	9. will
4. will	6. may	8. will	10. may

4

3. may (OR might) have an accident.
4. may (OR might) break.
5. may (OR might) not win.
6. may (OR might) get lost.
7. may (OR might) not live.
8. may (OR might) bite.

9. may (OR might) get sick.
10. may (OR might) close.

UNIT DESIRES, INVITATIONS, REQUESTS: *WOULD LIKE, WOULD YOU LIKE . . . ?, WOULD YOU PLEASE . . . ?*

❶

1. At the bus station.   3. At a movie theater.
2. On an airplane.

❷

3. Sheila would like to talk to you.
4. Would your parents like to come?
5. Sandy and Billy would like some coffee.
6. Would Dan like to come with us?
7. My friend and I would like a table for two.
8. Would the teacher like to come to the party?
9. I would like to take a long trip.
10. We would like you to have dinner with us.

❸

2. Ari would like Conchita to bring the CDs.
3. Ari would like Irene and Amira to help with the cooking.
4. Ari would like Eric to bring his CD player.
5. Ari would like Harry, Mike, and Tom to move the furniture.
6. Ari would like Ellen to buy some ice cream.
7. Ari would like Victor to pick up the birthday cake.
8. Ari would like Carmen and Ted to keep Tony busy.
9. Ari would like Ratana to make the decorations.

❹

2. Would you like
3. Would you like
4. would like
5. Would you like me to give
6. What would you like to do
7. Where would you like to go
8. Would you like to go
9. Would you like to see
10. What time would you like to go
11. would like to get
12. Where would you like to eat

❺

2. Would (OR Could) you (please) give me the key to my room?
3. Would (OR Could) you (please) explain the meaning of the word *grateful?*
4. Would (OR Could) you (please) give me change for a dollar?
5. Would (OR Could) you (please) take a picture of me and my friends?
6. Would (OR Could) you (please) take me to the airport?
7. Would (OR Could) you (please) help me with my suitcases?
8. Would (OR Could) you (please) show me the brown shoes in the window?
9. Would (OR Could) you (please) sit down?

PART COMPARISONS; THE PAST PROGRESSIVE

UNIT 38 COMPARATIVE FORM OF ADJECTIVES

❶

✓ — 2, 3, 5, 7

❷

One Syllable — fast, high, hot, long, old, small
Two Syllables — crowded, easy, friendly, heavy, messy, noisy, pretty
Three or Four Syllables — dangerous, difficult, expensive, intelligent

❸

2. better
3. farther
4. more intelligent
5. worse
6. messier
7. more comfortable
8. more careful
9. prettier
10. more difficult
11. easier

❹

2. longer than
3. more expensive than
4. bigger than
5. higher than
6. hotter than
7. more dangerous than
8. more crowded than
9. noisier than
10. heavier than
11. faster than
12. friendlier than

5

2. Is this unit easier OR more difficult than the last unit? It is more difficult. (OR It is easier.)
3. Is this watch cheaper OR more expensive than that watch? It is cheaper.
4. Are you younger OR older than your best friend? I am younger (OR I am older.)
5. Are you taller OR shorter than your teacher? I am taller. (OR I am shorter.)
6. Is your hometown bigger OR smaller than Los Angeles? It is smaller. (OR It is bigger.)
7. Is today's weather better OR worse than yesterday's weather? It is better. (OR It is worse.)

UNIT **ADVERBS OF MANNER AND COMPARATIVE FORMS OF ADVERBS**

1

3. adverb
4. adjective
5. adverb
6. adverb
7. adverb
8. adjective
9. adjective
10. adverb
11. adverb
12. adjective

2

B	H	A	P	P	I	L	Y		F
A	E	A	S	I	L	Y		Q	A
D	A	N	G	E	R	O	U	S	L	Y
L	V	G						I	T
Y	I	R	P	A	T	I	E	N	T	L	Y
	L	I						T	
	Y	L		W	E	L	L		
		Y						Y	

3

2. quietly
3. dangerously
4. angrily
5. happily
6. well
7. badly
8. fast
9. patiently
10. easily

4

2. beautiful, beautiful
3. fast, fast
4. tired, tired
5. well, good
6. carefully, careful
7. loud, loudly (OR loud)
8. angrily, angry
9. easy, easily

5

2. harder
3. better
4. more carefully
5. faster
6. more neatly
7. worse
8. more quickly
9. more easily
10. higher
11. more rudely

UNIT **ADJECTIVE + *ENOUGH* / *TOO* / *VERY*; *AS* + *ADJECTIVE* / *ADVERB* + *AS***

1

2. f
3. h
4. c
5. a
6. d
7. e
8. g

2

2. The apartment is too small for six people.
3. Shirley and Jack are too slow to run in the race.
4. The car is too expensive for us to buy.
5. The children are too young to start school.
6. The room is too cold.

3

2. The jacket isn't big enough for me.
3. The break wasn't long enough.
4. It isn't light enough to take a picture.
5. It isn't quiet enough to talk.
6. Buses aren't fast enough.

4

2. too
3. too
4. very
5. very
6. too
7. very
8. very
9. too

5

2. This coffee is too strong to drink.
3. The instructions were too difficult to understand.
4. The fruit is not ripe enough to eat.
5. The line is too long to wait.
6. The sweater was too dirty to wash by hand.
7. He is not rich enough to marry.
8. The eggs are cooked enough to eat.

6

3. too frightened
4. not big enough
5. too late
6. hot enough
7. too tight
8. too short
9. not safe enough
10. warm enough
11. not sunny enough

7

✓ — 2, 3, 4, 6, 7

8

3. as
4. than
5. as
6. than
7. as
8. as
9. as
10. than
11. than
12. than

9

4. Trains aren't as fast as airplanes.
5. January is as cold as February.
6. The chair is as comfortable as the sofa.
7. The governor of Oregon isn't as famous as the president of the United States.
8. The bank isn't as far as the post office.
9. Limes are as sour as lemons.
10. Jazz is more relaxing than rock music.
11. Chocolate ice cream isn't as good as vanilla ice cream.
12. Some people are more violent than other people.
13. College isn't as easy as high school.
14. These boxes are as heavy as those boxes.

10

2. Are you the same height as your brother?
3. Is your mother the same age as your father?
4. Is the dining room the same size as the living room?
5. Are the apples the same price as the oranges?
6. Are you the same weight as your brother?
7. Is *War and Peace* the same length as *Crime and Punishment*?
8. Is the subway station the same distance as the bus stop?

11

3. A bike is the same as a bicycle.
4. A TV is the same as a television.
5. North America is different from the United States.
6. 10,362 is different from 10.362.
7. 3 × 16 is the same as 16 × 3.
8. 16 ÷ 3 is different from 3 ÷ 16.
9. $1 is different from £1.
10. A snack bar is different from a restaurant.
11. 12:00 P.M. is the same as noon.
12. A plane is the same as an airplane.

UNIT THE PAST PROGRESSIVE

1

(Answers will vary.)

2

2. She was talking on the phone.
3. They were waiting for a table.
4. They were studying.

5. She was typing.
6. He was buying some groceries.
7. She was taking a shower.
8. She was cooking dinner.
9. He was getting gas.
10. He was going to school.

3

3. wasn't reading
4. were waiting
5. weren't standing
6. was wearing
7. wasn't holding
8. wasn't buying
9. weren't leaving

4

2. While my father was talking to me, someone rang the doorbell.
3. The boys were playing basketball when the fight started.
4. I was swimming when I got a pain in my leg.
5. When we saw the accident, we were driving down Market Street.
6. The doctor was examining Mrs. May when she screamed.
7. While I was washing my hair, I got some soap in my eyes.
8. Alan was shaving when he cut himself.
9. The train came while we were getting our tickets.

5

2. Was he meeting with his salespeople
3. Was she teaching
4. Was he swimming
5. Was she practicing the piano
6. Was he listening to a business report on the radio
7. Were they having dinner
8. Were they watching the news
9. Was she taking a bath

6

1b. hurried
2a. was watching
2b. answered
3a. were sleeping
3b. ran
4a. were standing
4b. sat
5a. was climbing
5b. called
6a. was ironing
6b. put

7

2. What were you doing? (OR Why were you standing there?)
3. What were you waiting for?
4. Where were you going?
5. Why were you going to the gym?
6. Who was driving?
7. How fast was he going (OR driving)?
8. Why was he driving (OR going) so fast?
9. Who was riding?

PART XI MODALS II; THE SUPERLATIVE

UNIT 42 SHOULD, SHOULDN'T, OUGHT TO, HAD BETTER, AND HAD BETTER NOT

1

2. shouldn't
3. should
4. shouldn't
5. shouldn't
6. should
7. should
8. shouldn't
9. should
10. shouldn't

2

2. I ought to visit my grandparents more often.
3. All passengers ought to arrive at the airport an hour before their flight.
4. Carol ought to study harder.
5. We ought to take something to the party.

3

2. You should cook the meat a little longer.
3. Lulu should be nicer to Elenore.
4. I should learn how to type.
5. Pete and Elenore should move into a smaller apartment.

4

2. should look for another one
3. shouldn't smoke
4. should go to the dentist
5. should wash it
6. shouldn't leave a tip
7. should study more
8. should leave early
9. shouldn't watch it
10. shouldn't touch it

5

2. Why should we have
3. How many (people) should we invite?
4. Who should we invite?
5. What should we buy?
6. What should we cook?
7. Where should we get
8. What should we do?
9. When should we send

6

a. 2, 5
b. 7, 10
c. 6
d. 4, 9
e. 3, 8

7

2. had better not serve shrimp
3. had better get a couple of bottles
4. had better not let the dog in the house
5. had better ask Costas to bring her
6. had better not sit together at the table
7. had better invite him
8. had better rent a video
9. had better borrow some from the neighbors

UNIT 43 HAVE TO, DON'T HAVE TO, MUST, MUSTN'T

1

(Answers will vary.)

2

2. have to, don't have to
3. don't have to, have to
4. have to, don't have to
5. don't have to, have to
6. have to, don't have to
7. don't have to, have to
8. have to, don't have to
9. have to, don't have to
10. don't have to, have to

3

2. has to leave early today.
3. have to go food shopping today.
4. have to come by taxi.
5. doesn't have to work late today.
6. don't have to clean up their room.
7. has to take some medicine.
8. don't have to pay for the tickets.
9. has to wear a suit and tie this morning.
10. doesn't have to do housework.

4

2. don't have to do the last exercise again.
3. didn't have to go to school yesterday.
4. had to clean her room yesterday.
5. doesn't have to write her parents every week.
6. didn't have to go shopping last week.
7. have to take tests.
8. don't have to buy a new car.
9. has to see her doctor today.
10. have to check my answers to this exercise.

5

2. You must stop.
3. You mustn't turn right.
4. You mustn't turn left.

5. You mustn't drive faster than 55 mph.
6. You mustn't park in this area.
7. You mustn't make a U-turn.
8. You mustn't pass.
9. You must go more slowly.

6

2. They had to find someone to take care of their dog.
3. They had to get to the airport on time.
4. They didn't have to get up early every morning.
5. They didn't have to go to work.
6. They had to look for a hotel.
7. They didn't have to make the bed every morning.
8. They had to pack and unpack suitcases.
9. They had to pay their hotel bill.
10. They didn't have to wash dishes.

7

2. Does your mother have to get up at 6:00 in the morning? Yes, she does. (OR No, she doesn't.)
3. Did you have to cook last night? Yes, I did. (OR No, I didn't.)
4. Does your best friend have to do this exercise? Yes, he / she does. (OR No, he / she doesn't.)
5. Do you have to be in English class on time? Yes, I do. (OR No, I don't.)
6. Do your friends have to learn English? Yes, they do. (OR No, they don't.)
7. Did your father have to shave yesterday? Yes, he did. (OR No, he didn't.)
8. Did your best friend have to go to work yesterday? Yes, he / she did. (OR No, he / she didn't.)
9. Did you have to take a test last week? Yes, I did. (OR No, I didn't.)

8

2. does she have to get a book from the library?
3. does he have to go?
4. did the teacher have to talk to?
5. did you have to stay there?
6. do the students have to stay after class?
7. do you have to use?
8. did the high school students have to send their college applications?
9. do you have to get up?
10. did he have to borrow?

UNIT **SUPERLATIVE FORM OF ADJECTIVES AND ADVERBS**

2. Doug   4. Carol   6. Carol
3. Norma   5. Norma

2. the worst   8. the ugliest
3. the hardest   9. the most popular
4. the most beautiful 10. the lowest
5. the busiest   11. the fastest
6. the funniest   12. the most charming
7. the best

(Answers for part b of each question will vary.)
2a. A teenager is the oldest of the three.
2b. A child is older than a baby.
3a. A Rolls Royce is the most expensive of the three.
3b. A BMW is more expensive than a Ford.
4a. Nigeria is the hottest of the three.
4b. Spain is hotter than Sweden.
5a. A highway is the widest of the three.
5b. A street is wider than a path.
6a. A city is the biggest of the three.
6b. A town is bigger than a village.
7a. An elephant is the heaviest of the three.
7b. A gorilla is heavier than a fox.
8a. An hour is the longest of the three.
8b. A minute is longer than a second.
9a. Boxing is the most dangerous of the three.
9b. Soccer is more dangerous than golf.
10a. Chocolate is the most fattening of the three.
10b. A banana is more fattening than a carrot.

4

1b. Andy came the earliest.
2a. The red car is going the most slowly (OR the slowest).
2b. The white car is going the fastest.
3a. Fran drives the most dangerously.
3b. Shirley drives the most carefully.
4a. Gary works the closest to his home.
4b. Harris works the farthest from his home.
5a. Carolyn speaks Spanish the best.
5b. Milton speaks Spanish the worst.
6a. Renée types the most quickly (OR the quickest).
6b. Joan types the most accurately.

PUTTING IT ALL TOGETHER

REVIEW OF VERB TENSES AND MODALS

2. We <u>are having</u> a wonderful time on our honeymoon.
3. Venice <u>is</u> such a romantic place
4. It <u>has</u> so many beautiful places.
5. Yesterday, we <u>walked</u> all around the city.
6. We <u>visited</u> several churches.
7. They <u>were</u> so wonderful

8. we <u>saw</u> so many gorgeous paintings
9. we <u>didn't go</u> far from our hotel
10. This afternoon, we <u>had</u> lunch
11. We both <u>ate</u> special Venetian dishes
12. Dan <u>is</u> resting
13. we <u>are going to</u> take a gondola ride

2

2. Where is their hotel?
3. What are they going to do tonight?
4. Why did they stay in their hotel last night?
5. Where are they going today?
6. What time will the tour start?
7. What is Dan doing?
8. Who is the tour guide?
9. Where are they going to have dinner (in the evening)?
10. Who are they going to have dinner with?
11. When did Carol and Dan meet two people from Canada?
12. What are the two people's names?
13. How long are Paul and Myra going to stay in Venice?
14. Who does Carol like a lot?
15. Why was Dan sick all night?
16. What does Dan love to do?

3

2. a	5. b	8. b	11. a
3. a	6. b	9. a	
4. a	7. b	10. b	

REVIEW OF VERB TENSES AND COMPARISONS

1

2. Teacher A is more organized than Teacher B.
3. Teacher A is nicer than Teacher B.
4. Teacher A teaches better than Teacher B.
5. Teacher A speaks more clearly than Teacher B.
6. Teacher A is friendlier than Teacher B.
7. Teacher A gives back homework more quickly than Teacher B.
8. Teacher A explains things more slowly than Teacher B.
9. The atmosphere in Teacher A's class is more relaxed than the atmosphere in Teacher B's class.
10. The homework in Teacher A's class is easier than the homework in Teacher B's class.
11. The books in Teacher A's class are more interesting than the books in Teacher B's class.
12. Unfortunately, the tests in Teacher A's class are harder than the tests in Teacher B's class.

2

2. Teacher B isn't as organized as Teacher A.
3. Teacher B isn't as nice as Teacher A.

4. Teacher B doesn't teach as well as Teacher A.
5. Teacher B doesn't speak as clearly as Teacher A.
6. Teacher B isn't as friendly as Teacher A.
7. Teacher B doesn't give back homework as quickly as Teacher A.
8. Teacher B doesn't explain things as slowly as Teacher A.
9. The atmosphere in Teacher B's class isn't as relaxed as the atmosphere in Teacher A's class.
10. The homework in Teacher B's class isn't as easy as the homework in Teacher A's class.
11. The books in Teacher B's class aren't as interesting as the books in Teacher A's class.
12. The tests in Teacher B's class aren't as hard as the tests in Teacher A's class.

REVIEW OF VERB TENSES, NOUNS, AND QUANTIFIERS

2. There are a few glasses in the first picture, but there are a lot of glasses in the second picture.
3. There are a lot of flowers in the first picture, but there are a few flowers in the second picture.
4. There is a lot of Coke in the first picture, but there is a little Coke in the second picture.
5. There is a little chocolate in the first picture, but there is a lot of chocolate in the second picture.
6. There are a few candles on the cake in the first picture, but there are a lot of candles on the cake in the second picture.
7. There is a lot of fruit in the first picture, but there is a little fruit in the second picture.
8. There is a lot of cheese in the first picture, but there is a little cheese in the second picture.
9. There is a little bread in the first picture, but there is a lot of bread in the second picture.
10. There are a few gifts in the first picture, but there are a lot of gifts in the second picture.

2

2. Is there much bread? No, there isn't.
3. Is there much butter? No, there isn't.
4. Are there many chairs? Yes, there are.
5. Is there much cheese? Yes, there is.
6. Is there much chocolate? No, there isn't.
7. Are there many flowers? Yes, there are.
8. Is there much fruit? Yes, there is.
9. Are there many gifts? No, there aren't.
10. Are there many glasses? No, there aren't.
11. Is there much orange juice? Yes, there is.
12. Are there many potato chips? Yes, there are.